BELIEVING

Books by Eugene C. Kennedy

Eugene C. Kennedy

BELIEVING

1974

DOUBLEDAY & COMPANY, INC., GARDEN CITY, NEW YORK

ISBN: 0-385-07496-4
Library of Congress Catalog Card Number 73-79681
Copyright © 1973, 1974 by Eugene C. Kennedy

CONTENTS

INTRODUCTION   7

I. BELIEVING

Chapter One: BELIEVING   13

Chapter Two: BELIEVE IT OR NOT:
     THE LANGUAGE OF BELIEVING   23

Chapter Three: INSIDE BELIEF   35

Chapter Four: INCARNATIONAL FAITH   47

Chapter Five: DOUBTING   64

Chapter Six: THE FACES OF FIDELITY   76

II. BELIEVERS

THEODORE HESBURGH   88

EUGENE MCCARTHY   99

ANN LANDERS   113

DALE FRANCIS   122

B. F. SKINNER   134

JAMES SHANNON   147

A MAN AND A WOMAN   158

JAMES EDWARD WALSH   166

III. WHAT DO I BELIEVE?

FAITH AND LIFE   179

CREATIVE FAITH   196

WHAT DO I BELIEVE IN?   207

I am writing this book to reflect on the problem of believing and to allow some other persons the opportunity to share their ideas and experiences of believing with those who read these pages. Believing is a traditional concern for anybody interested in religion or in life; indeed, believing is a profoundly human characteristic, a note by which men and women are defined and distinguished from other species. We do not have a choice about believing any more than we do about breathing, and each is equally important for our survival. What and how we believe provide other questions which, as we know from history and psychology, we continue to answer in a wide variety of ways. The inclusion of a section of interviews with persons representing sharply different traditions reflects this truth.

Believing is a problem for the theologian on a theoretical level, but it is a practical one for all of us on an everyday level. During the course of some research on American priests conducted a few years ago I became aware of how hard it is for most people to speak clearly about what they believe *in*. It is far simpler to describe what we believe *about*. Perhaps that tells us something of the abstract way in which we have been instructed in the articles of faith or it may merely give further testimony to our difficulty in putting deeply personal meanings into words. That last task is one of the functions of the symbolism and language of believing. It may be that we are so estranged from a religious language that speaks effectively to and of our experience that we resemble strangers in a foreign land— limited in our capacity to express our faith not because of a failure to believe but because we lack the language in which to do it effectively. To explore the nature and function of believing in the personality and to find the words and signs that enable men and women to sense and sing of the richness of their need and power to believe is perhaps the dominant religious challenge of the age. I think that this book helps to define that challenge rather than to answer it; it provides, I hope, a sense of direction for all of us who are concerned with the meaning of life and with providing a Christian vision of it to searching mankind.

The book is divided into three sections. In the first part, I attempt to reflect on the nature of believing in the lives of men and women. Although I reviewed the literature of psychological research in preparation for this task, I have placed it in the context of the convictions about the need to believe which have grown in me as I have been privileged to work closely with many different human persons. To argue for the central significance of believing may seem as conventional as defending baseball, the flag, and mother love. If you think about it for a moment, however, there has been a great deal of argument about even these formerly unquestioned aspects of our heritage. So it is with believing which has been drained of some of its full-bodied vigor through the long and almost unconscious historical process by which beliefs have come to be defined in terms of dogmas and other intellectual statements. Faith is a function of the person rather than of just a part of him; men and women are eager to believe, but they want something substantial to give themselves to, something that matches their joys and sorrows, something that sounds a call to believe deeply rather than just to close their eyes and hold on to some old-time religion.

The second section contains a non-representational sample of interviews with a number of people who represent very differing views and religious traditions. Some of them have abandoned their own religious profession but they have not given up on believing. Everybody believes in some framework or explanatory system, some philosophy or scheme of purpose. In many cases what those of us who profess the Christian creed may find is that what we actively believe *in*—that is to say, the set of beliefs that we build our lives on—needs further honest exploration on our part. People do not like to examine their belief system too closely for fear that they will find too many inconsistencies or that they may be tempted to reject articles of their religious creed, and they do not want to do this. That leaves our faith somewhat vague or in the uneasy adjustment of never being integrated with our life experience. This section, in which these persons speak for themselves, may encourage us to look at our own lives and the things we say we believe in; we can only do that for ourselves. The outcome of such a search of ourselves need not be frightening; in fact, it is essential if our faith is to remain fresh and active. To keep matching our experience and our beliefs with each other in order to draw them more closely together—in order to achieve the wholeness that living faith does provide—is an essential religious action.

In order to carry this out, we need the assistance of organized religion; we need a Church sensitive to the human struggle to believe which speaks not only the truths of faith to us but which joins with us as we seek to express our faith. One of the purposes of this book is to reinforce the importance of the institutional Church and to discuss its opportunities positively rather than to criticize it for its failings. We have come to the end of the age of romantic renewal and what lies before all of us is the hard work of providing the pastoral and liturgical responses that will give a Christian sense of meaning and purpose back to the world. I think that the belief needs of men and women run painfully deep and that the Church that understands what it believes in can provide the sacramental environment and the human community in which faith can come vigorously to life for them.

Recently, in an interview with psychologist Carl Rogers he

told me that he has come to believe that he is wiser than his intellect, that he knows more than he knows. He referred to levels of understanding and response that are deep within his total personality. I think the same phrases can be applied to the Church which has learned so much of which it is hardly aware during its long life with mankind. It is wiser than it knows; it has depths of understanding and a consciousness that has absorbed the symbols and myths of a hundred cultures. It knows more of the language of faith than it permits itself to speak; the Church needs to believe more in its own creative capacity to bring forth new things and old from its treasure of human religious experience. The black psychiatrist Franz Fanon is quoted by psychologist Rollo May as saying that America should export poets rather than weapons and machinery to the developing countries of Africa. As May notes, this is because poets can communicate on a level that enables all men to recognize each other as brothers; when they can communicate they can also build community. In the matter of believing, I think the Church has poetic resources that it needs to free once more in behalf of the developing faith of mankind. This very rich fullness of the Church's ability to hear and respond to the human search for faith is its prime resource; it has nothing to fear in believing that it can speak with meanings deeper than it knows itself. The Church believes more than it believes literally, and the opportunities to share all this with mankind are surely present.

In the last section of this book I briefly attempt to integrate what I learned while writing it and to share some of the things in which I truly believe. Having finished this book, I realize how much more there is to write on the subject; this is, then, a beginning at best but one that I hope will help others to look at and understand their own beliefs more fully.

EUGENE C. KENNEDY,

F.S.

I

BELIEVING

Chapter One

BELIEVING

"I believe in America." So begins the folk tale of our age as the suppliant wax mustached undertaker presents his request for a favor to the godfather. He is a true believer in the classic and familiar mold, the patient and hopeful man who had come to a golden and fair America. This was the land where things got better for immigrants from countries where things kept getting worse, the place that would be believed in because hard work and patience were ultimately rewarded. It is a worldly-wise kind of belief, of course, one that is untroubled by its acceptance of evil in the nature of things. The little man believes in exchanged indebtedness, of pacts as ancient as the land he came from. He believes, most of all, in the godfather.

"I'd like to say I believe," intones the anguished celebrant in Leonard Bernstein's "Mass." This is the voice of the troubled and sensitive man, well educated but torn in his own conscience about the problem of believing. He is uncomfortable with the evil he cannot explain or do away with, and he cannot resolve the conflict that will not stay asleep. He is far removed from the confident immigrant who puts his faith in the Mafiadom. He is more typical of modern men caught up in the profound anguish of wanting and needing to believe but uncertain of how to express or experience it. You can feel something dying in them as something else struggles for life, a search or a bridge firm enough to hold them as they move on in the journey of life.

Both of these persons illustrate very differing aspects of our human need to believe. Belief has been looked on as something that helps us triumph over the natural, of virtue that strengthens us to assent to explaining systems of truth. Because belief has come to seem a test of virtue we have practically lost sight of how natural believing is for all men. We are more familiar with the sudden willingness to believe in God that is discovered in foxholes, a kind of belief, long resisted, but finally accepted by the repentant sinner. Believing has been the dramatic device pitting the man of religion against the man of science, the all or nothing kind of phenomenon that admitted little curiosity and few questions about its content. We may just be recovering from the notion of believing as a duty imposed by authority, one made ultimately more rewarding for us if we go along with it against all doubts and wonders.

It is hard for us to focus on believing as a healthy and quite normal human activity that always co-exists with questioning and uncertainty. It is impossible for man to understand or fully humanize himself without being a believing person. Too often the question of what he believes—especially if framed in the language of a certain period of time—has obscured the essential role that active believing plays in his life. Furious battles have raged around what man should believe as they have about how and when he ought to believe. One does not necessarily make light of the content of belief to observe the number of pennants that have fluttered over the battlefields strewn with the corpses of differing true believers. Making war over beliefs is surely a sign of how important the activity of believing has always been to human beings; it is a tragedy, however, when this elementary human inclination is shriveled and scorched by the unknowing flames of controversy. Putting belief in a vise is a mistake because it goes against what we understand about all other human functions. There is nothing locked in about man, no way in which he will ever hear or utter the last word on any issue in his life. Believing will always retain notes of searching in the healthy person who feels constrained and crippled if his spontaneous response is choked by too many rigid or irreducible formulations.

The latter maneuver is the action of fearful and uncertain persons, like the archbishop of a great archdiocese who, with the urbanity and charm found in a special way among the successful Irish, introduced me at a lecture series once with a preface about the accomplishments of the Second Vatican Council. Just before I was to begin, however, his voice grew quieter, as though his vocal cords sat tense in anticipation of the solemn words he was about to speak. He was a modern godfather, it seemed to me, reminding the family of how it functioned. "My dear people, you must remember that no matter how many fine speakers you hear, the bishops are the only true teachers in the Church." This kind of remark has become almost a caricature for the administrative churchman who feels that orthodox beliefs are always in danger and must not be looked at too closely, much less tampered with. The same archbishop, in fact, told a distinguished gathering of biblical scholars that the best thing they could do was to gather together and recite to themselves the Credo of Pope Paul VI. This is consistent with the approach which serves institutional but not personal ends. It may be very well for an organized Church, for complicated reasons, to be very protective of what it classifies as its content of beliefs. This is frequently very hard, however, on the believer who is urged to conform to the statements made by the institution even when these do not seem appropriate or helpful in his own life situation. There is an inevitable tension between institution and individual which has been well recognized over the last generation in the Catholic Church. The essence of dialogue has consisted, to some extent, in that space where believers have tried to search out the full dimensions of their beliefs in the shadows of the institution that finds it far more difficult to look searchingly at its statements on faith.

It remains true, however, that the person must believe in order to be himself. He is not inclined to be a disbeliever at any level of his activity. He has never rejected religion arbitrarily. It has more often been a painful and difficult

struggle rather than a malicious or prideful turning away
from what is called teaching authority. Man says in a thousand ways, "I would like to say I believe." It has been his
anguished cry throughout history as he has tried to understand and deepen his appreciation of the religious patterns
and symbols that have explained his life.

Believing becomes more difficult as authority insists on
precise requirements about the language, content, or conditions under which believing must be carried out, especially
if these fail to capture the current cultural mood or sense of
human search or longing. When these requirements simply
or in combination fail to match an individual's unique vision
of the world and his own experience, conflict begins to
build immediately. Man is confused when this occurs because his reaction seems to place him in conflict with those
people who are his teachers, the presumably wise and trustworthy authorities who profess concern about him, his life,
and his salvation. This searching believer seems pitted against
tradition which seems to resist his inquiries as improper;
actually he is merely experiencing an impulse to believe
more deeply. The person's problems with religious faith
arise not from an urge to disbelieve but from a passionate
need to believe as richly and profoundly as possible. Men
and women want to make sense out of life, and they do not
willingly put aside any system of teaching or any explanation that helps them in this regard. Persons believe in something even when they style themselves as unbelievers. The
latter word merely describes the fact that they can no longer
accept certain styles of creed or that they cannot honestly
respond to certain statements that are urged upon them as at
the heart and core of God's revelation. They are saying that
they cannot believe *that;* they are not saying that they cannot believe.

God has always been a problem for man, not so much
because of God but because of men who have made believing into such a complicated process. To believe is, nonetheless, as essential for man as air and water. Human beings

need to believe and to expand their capacity to invest themselves in other persons, in causes, and in the religious concepts that allow them to understand themselves and the universe. Believing is an essential human function without which he finds it almost impossible to understand or to integrate his personality. We should not be surprised to find that the phenomenon of believing, like all other human activity, can be snagged or frustrated, especially because of the complexities of man's emotional life. Man hungers to believe in order to have a sense of meaning and purpose; he wants to believe because of the soundings of his own spirit that howl and whisper alternately about his possibilities and his destiny. Men and women need to make some sense of our mostly unexceptional lives. Believing, with its past anchors and future referents, is not an easy task, nor is it one that is ever completely finished; nonetheless, we are all engaged in it despite the diversity of our activities or our professions. Whether we think about our belief or state it explicitly and try to preach it to others, we operate from some surround of meaning through which we justify what we do in life. The desire to believe, in other words, is everywhere to be observed even though its manifestations may seem irreligious or even anti-religious at times. What is important to recognize is the essential humanity of this quest for at least partial answers to life's problems, for some light as we make our way along its all too often dark passageways.

The evidence is not hard to discover. If there is one thing that young people have articulated, it is this human desire to believe. They have been telling us that they are in need of credible adults, persons they themselves can believe in, older individuals who can provide models on which they can base their own lives. As will be discussed later, this pursuit of belief, sometimes awkward and ill stated, is an integral part of human growth. Learning to believe, in other words, goes along with growing up. The person who has not developed some belief system to guide his life is probably not grown up in other areas as well. It may well be that the content and style of a person's belief reflect as well as anything else the character of the development of his over-all personality.

Some people believe in music, as a recently popular song put it, while others have tapped their data cards, checked their statistical tables, and told us that they rely on findings. Indeed, our willingness to accept scientific findings, especially if they are put into print, makes this a new age of faith. Scientific conclusions, after all, seem extraordinarily reliable. They provide a framework of meaning for the events of our lives in the same way that psychology and some of its off-shoots, such as the encounter group phenomenon, provide a sense of significance for others. There has probably never been a more rigidly orthodox set of beliefs than the tenets of psychoanalysis which, in some of the more grief-laden chapters of scientific history, has had its heretics and apostates as well as its true believers. Still others, in the fashion of previous generations, believe strongly in astrology and the influence of planetary movements on human affairs. Many presently believe in the movies, especially in the curious present age when the reproduction of life and sound on film or tape has provided almost a surrogate way of life for some. It is not surprising to hear the young and successful director Peter Bogdanovich, pale from a lack of sunshine, telling of how he spends most of his time watching movies, especially those made before he was born. He has become, in some ways, an exegete of American experience through the movies. These films constitute an environment of meaning and symbolism for him. Perhaps closely related are the people, many of them young, who seem to believe that the most exciting thing in life is to record and listen secondhand to a conversation they have just been engaged in. Is this strange electronic abstraction, a temporary offshoot of our gadgetry, a prophecy of a coming life dominated and conditioned by sophisticated communications that provide an illusion of living while holding life at a distance at the same time?

Great divergences exist among religious people, even within the same Church. The Roman Catholic Church serves as the classic example. It makes room for people who believe in very different ways while at the same time, and for the institutional purposes mentioned before, it holds itself together against the shuddering impact of the varying styles of its believers. Some Catholics believe persistently in wonders and a God who is somewhat stern and mindful of our slightest actions as he checks off our merits and demerits. Others see God as love and understanding and are far more casual in the way they believe and in the way they worship. Still others are struggling somewhere in the middle, not sure exactly what they believe any more, but aware, at some level at least, that they have a very real need to believe in something in order to survive. The challenge for religious organizations to contain and respond to such pressures is enormous.

There are those in life who believe in money or power, who profess a faith in bartering or buying what they conceive will be the most satisfying experiences of life. It may appear to be a sterile and isolating kind of faith, but it marshals together great energies and is a pivot for powerful achievements.

For some belief seems to be nothing but a memory, something mourned from an earlier period of life. Recollecting the time in which they put aside the only faith they ever knew, they speak in this way, "I used to believe that . . . when I was younger." These people survive with a need to believe to which an adequate response has not been made; they have not been helped with new or more appropriate statements or images of a faith to explain and give meaning to their lives. Occasionally sorrow tinges their voices even though they speak proudly of their liberation from what they judge to have been tyrannizing experiences of earlier religious faith. The traces of these previous beliefs, especially the echoes of the strong cultural setting in which they first heard them, are never erased from their souls. In this company one may number sensitive people who feel that they cannot go home again to that place where such simple things were once so utterly believable. They are searchers, painfully aware of their need for something to believe in and frequently carrying with them, as Irish Catholic writers often do, the imprints they sometimes count as scars of long gone beliefs. Such individuals have not given up on believing; they would respond readily to those who might speak to them with suitable sophistication and understanding about their own questions and the surprisingly complex nature of life as they have known it. Frequently they have lost belief in the institution of the Church because it seemed incapable of making room for them or of understanding their honest doubts about the beliefs it had urged upon them. Many contemporary people who have had good educations, if not the profound awareness of the creative artist, have come to question the ecclesiastical organization which has had such an influence on shaping the possibilities of their belief experience. They have listened to theologians talk of the demythologization of the scriptures. They have not been deaf to those who have talked reasonably about our need to reinterpret certain religious statements or teachings lest they be lost in an archaic language or style of presentation which no longer speak to present day experience or events. Some of these desire to believe, but they do not know quite what to believe in a time when certain aspects of Church teaching seem still very much in question. They know that they can neither accept nor believe rigid authoritarian statements, and they have been conditioned to think that this is the only alternative they would get from the institutional Church. Believing, for them, is a serious matter about which they may possess deep and revealing emotions. They do not want to stir the waters of faith which they perceive as muddy enough already. They do not want to push themselves to a point of unnecessary anguish or irrevocable decision against faith, and so they live in some twilight where they still believe even though they are not quite sure what they do believe in.

It is probably true that the arguments about faith have been quite far removed from the ordinary individual's experience. Something about theology textbooks and ecclesiastical decrees is intrinsically remote from the day-to-day struggle to understand oneself, to plumb the mysteries of friendship and love, and to try to live purposefully in a difficult and conflicting world. Perhaps believers need to be reintroduced to the process of believing as a natural, healthy, and quite resilient aspect of personality structure. The capacity to believe is intensely human. Strangely enough, it does not thrive when there is too much certainty or when all questioning is ruled out. Believing incorporates man into life and into relationships with others in a manner that matches their inherent imperfection and incompleteness. Belief is necessarily a membrane stretched across our vulnerability, fragile even when it is strong. It is related and depends on so many things that can shift or go wrong at almost any moment. Believing is a dynamic rather than a rigid quality. It expands and it contracts; it is more like breathing than holding one's breath. Believing cannot be activated by force or by fear. It arises from within us as a response to the situations, events, and symbols which we recognize as expressive of the truth of our lives; we believe in these when they are adequate to our experience, when they help disclose its meaning to us.

Perhaps we should look at what supports us in our simple relationships and work to identify human lynch pins of faith that hold the sections of our lives together. These may, at any given moment, seem fairly shaky; no one has ever seen God or been able to predict when or if death, illness, accident, or unexpected estrangement would smash the balance of experiences through which we express our beliefs. Faith is conditioned by and is tied up at each step with the world and people as we know them; faith first has a simple operational definition and only secondly one that is theologically abstract. Believing becomes clearer as we recognize its thousand faces in everyday life. Believing is what we live by.

The question centers not on what we should believe nor on what should we believe about; it is phrased far less dramatically but far more accurately as what do we believe in. This is a hard question because it is so much easier to recite a creed than it is to know and admit to ourselves just what it is that we count on or what are the bases for our important life decisions in our lives. We sometimes hesitate or actively resist exploring the actual philosophy or theology with which we operate in our everyday lives. Often this is marginally related at best to the creed we recite on Sundays; it manifests to us, however, as nothing else could, the real nature of our believing. Whether this is tentative or absolute, something mourned or something merely longed for, the mystery of believing is only understood when we get at the truth of what we believe in ourselves. Sometimes a kind of psychological archeology is needed to sift through the various deposits and artifacts that have piled up on this foundation during our lifetimes; at the bottom of the layers we come finally to a place where we can dig no deeper—where who we are and what we believe in, scraped clean of disguising debris, are laid bare at last.

Chapter Two

BELIEVE IT OR NOT: THE LANGUAGE OF
BELIEVING

The person can be defined as a believing phenomenon, as one who must believe in order to live at all. Believing is as fundamental as loving in the human situation but few songs and little poetry are written about it. Believing, in fact, seems to be the subject rather of exhortation than celebration. You are free to love, but you must believe. Man has experienced such an imperative about belief that he has only slowly come to inspect it as his means of tapping into and freely symbolizing his identity and the meaning of his universe.

We speak casually of the fact that some things are easy and other things are harder to believe. That is not so much a statement about the relative truth of these objects of belief as it is a reflection of the psychological difficulties involved in committing oneself to a certain way of looking at the world. We speak in a similar way of people who have weak faith or strong faith; again we describe the inner state of the individuals rather than anything about the quality or even the character of what they believe in. We have an assorted vocabulary for discussing our inner passion to believe; it is that inner urge and need to believe that helps us to recognize ourselves as human. For all our talk, we still only approximate an understanding of this essential human activity.

We have had, for example, the traditional philosophical and theological approaches to the nature of belief, some of them magnificent in their explorations, within the possibilities of their own discipline, of the believing activity of man. Most of these reflections, however, are unavailable in any adequate translation for the average person. He or she recognizes, without instruction in the matter, that the language of belief is largely one of symbols and myths, poetic imagery that reaches by routes unknown the deep layers of his being. The philosophical and theological analysis of faith is, for the average individual, too remote and frequently too dry. Despite the testimony it gives to the anguish of the researchers who produce it academic faith quickly becomes too abstract from the everyday experience of humanity. If you have ever heard a sermon preached by a philosophically minded clergyman to a relatively unsophisticated audience, you will appreciate instantly the gulf that separates the trained mind (which might relish the reasoning involved) from the generally disinterested response of the hearers who are absorbed with the problems of living. It is not that they do not want to learn about their faith; rather they do not think about their experiences easily in the categories of philosophical or theological abstraction. Sometimes they cannot even recognize the faith they do possess when it comes in that form. Talk about belief is just not the same as believing.

Believing has also been approached by the social sciences and psychiatry. Most people understand that Sigmund Freud perceived religion as a neurotic outcropping from man's permanent sense of his own helplessness. Religion, in this view, is a regressive phenomenon which does not serve man's integration nor in any way speak to the perfection of his personality. Many psychiatrists and theologians have rightly disagreed with this oversimplification, but it cannot be denied that this attitude has had a powerful effect on the estrangement of organized religion from the human sciences. Freud clearly offered a belief system of his own; he felt that if persons recognized the unconscious origins of their own activities they could be freed from the magical interpretations of the universe which the distorted religion he saw in his practice had offered to man. This battle against traditional religion is not at an end despite the fact that many social scientists and psychiatrists have worked toward achieving a cease fire and a measure of peaceful co-existence with theologians. A recent restatement of Freudian theory by Weston LaBarre[1] challenges this rapprochement vigorously, claiming in effect that the compromising social scientists are encouraging human beings to turn back toward an infantile interpretation of their world.

The social scientists of religion, chiefly anthropologists and sociologists, have provided brilliant analyses of the functional nature of believing in the history and life of mankind. They have not dealt with the essential nature of belief as much as with its sociological reality; they have observed in detail not only religion's persistence but also a pervasive human need for religious interpretive systems in order to make life livable at all. The symbol systems of religion, to risk a shorthand version of their research, offer man a way of looking at and comprehending his own existence and the activities, including those that are contradictory and inimical to safety, of life around him. Man is particularly fragile and dependent on effective symbols in order to interact with other men and with this somewhat hostile universe around him. He needs myths that are well fashioned in order to preserve the truths which, like air and water for his physical life, enable him to manage his way through history with a personal sense of continuity and significance. The social scientists record the fact of believing and describe quite accurately its function even when they do not speculate about the specific content of its varied doctrines. Indeed, an observer as acute as Robert Bellah[2] suggests that, solely on the basis of the powerful functions which religion fulfills for man, it possesses a special kind of truth. This exists irrespective of the truth or falsity of any of the doctrines of any of the faiths that have in any way been provided for mankind. Bellah's message is that humans must believe be-

---

[1] *The Ghost Dance* (Garden City: Doubleday & Company, Inc., 1970).

[2] *Beyond Belief* (New York: Harper & Row, 1970).

yond belief, that they must exercise their capacity to believe even when they cannot believe in the literal doctrines of their particular faith. Believing, he says, is good for you no matter what you believe in. Believing is so essential, in his view, that it must be reinforced or the structure of life as we know it starts to come unglued.

The research of social scientists reveals believing as a perennial function that is essential for man's survival; without it he will collapse in the face of life's inequities. They have lighted up the deep roots of belief and have helped us to understand symbols and myths as essential food for believing persons. Indeed, the social science research has refurbished the meaning of myth for modern persons so they have come to appreciate anew that myths are not fables or deceptive stories. Religious myth is an enduring mode of communication through which essential notes about man himself are transmitted across the generations. The social scientists have given man back the keys to the language of believing, an understanding of myths as bearers of the things the human person does not want to forget about himself, including his ideals and the conditions he needs for growth and development. Myths provide the stories in which we can identify our own story and understand its meaning.

The recognition that myth is the language of believing has enabled scripture scholars to reinvestigate the Bible and to tell again its magnificent stories without the penalty of literalness, which made believing increasingly difficult for educated and scientific minds. This demythologization of the scriptures has had extensive reverberations in theology and, more recently, in the ordinary life of Christians who, frequently without much preparation, have suddenly seen and heard their familiar faith myths juggled and transformed. The living language of poetry has been presented again to the believer as the proper language of faith. The old historical and narrow interpretation has, howsoever urgently, been put aside. This has led to a revolution in teaching and understanding the content and meaning of faith. This enterprise is by no means concluded and the practical effects of restaging the epical themes of man's beliefs in modern times continue to cause anguish, disappointment, and disillusionment to those persons who have been instructed in a rigid interpretation of historical faith. The conflict between the literalists and those trying to offer a renewal interpretation—in effect a more believable holy writ—has not yet subsided. Battle smoke rises yet above the various Church groups where fire and thunder have surrounded this new exploration of the meaning of myth and its central role as the language through which the believer understands and speaks.

In other words, in great numbers persons have reclaimed a feeling for the essentially human intuitive processes through which religious truths have been preserved in our consciousness throughout history. There are, it would seem, spiritual capacities in human beings which awaken without elaborate instruction in the presence of profound symbols and myths. This is not basically a rational process, and it can neither be planned nor activated by intellectual means or mathematical procedures. The great souls of each century hear the special new music that sings again of the basic materials of belief; they respond to it and, without quite knowing what they are doing, they help the rest of us to understand it through the symbols—artistic, cinematic, liturgical—which they fashion for us. These sensitive souls are always processing the experience at the borders of our awareness and calling back to us so that we can follow them forward. It is difficult to recapture a sense of the poetic as *the* language of faith precisely because the unpoetic have tried to express faith in hard and fast creedal statements for centuries. They have tried to freeze isolated moments in the long story of human awareness and to mark these off as the approved and sacred quadrants of belief. This has proved not only deathly to poets but almost deathly to faith and the act of believing as well. It is one of the reasons that the learned theologian can be so far from human experience while the unlettered and the loving can provide us with such a clear sense of living faith. Very simple people respond more poetically—that is, free of the need for rational order but sure of their theological sense of direction—than many trained scholars who have been separated from the gutty business of living.

This is not to say that faith is irrational; it is, however, to recognize that it is a response of the total person and that, as such, it has always expressed itself best in the most abiding personal language we know, that of myth and poetry. It may be hard to define a dogma in this language just as it would be to write an equation. Defining a profound religious truth in the exact language of any one age may, however, not be as vital to believing as one might have supposed. Faith as a self-renewing source of life across the centuries; faith as the convictions or the sense of believers; faith as a way of looking at and inserting oneself into life: these may be perennially poetic aspects of believing that could not otherwise communicate themselves to men.

The decline of dogma may be related to the contemporary person's rejection of non-mythic categories far more than a rejection of believing. It is clear that the rediscovery of the special language of belief has estranged us for the moment from the exclusively literal approach to faith. But we have been so constrained poetically that we are only beginning to sensitize ourselves to its special communication—and we do not yet recognize the signs and symbols that are already there all around us, speaking of what we must believe in order to be saved. They will be recognized by the poets of faith who will yet arise—and they are already arising in the arts around us—and who will teach us this language again.

We are in a period of waiting, where worn-down literalism no longer appeals to man but where new symbols and poetry have yet to be recognized and incorporated in the life of the Church or our other institutions.

When literal biblical beliefs could no longer be accepted without question men felt estranged from a rich and stable part of their cultural heritage. They had been denied the concepts through which they had imposed meaning on their world and, such was their bitter wisdom, they knew they could never take them up again. Persons who are estranged from their ineffective literalism and who are not yet in possession of a newer and fresher symbol find that real changes can take place in the mode and object of their belief systems. Believing has not passed out of fashion; it has, however, emerged in disguised ways for some persons. Jan Ehrenwald, a New York psychiatrist, has suggested that the sudden flourishing of the occult is a symptom of what he calls "myth-deprivation." In other words, when people are denied their heroes or the simple stories, such as the literal understanding of Adam and Eve, they encounter great difficulties in believing as they once did. They continue to believe, however, because they are impelled to search for something to make sense out of what they know in the world around them. In the interlude between the death of old myths and the birth of new ones, man must believe in something. Ehrenwald suggests that many persons turn to the negative image of traditional believing, to an embrace of superstition, devil worship, and other such activities. These do not constitute a sign of evil rampant as much as they provide evidences of the human need to believe and the urgent nature of the search for the believable.

Ehrenwald compares the sudden explosion of interest in the occult to the irrational and sometimes psychoticlike behavior of individuals who are deprived of their dreams in the course of sleep research. It has been noted that if experimental subjects are awakened just as they begin to dream—if, in other words, their dreams are denied them—they suffer from this loss in very obvious ways. Dreams apparently are not random events but a type of inner myth that integrates the varied experiences of our day. Dreams do this in a semi-poetic fashion, using symbolism and condensation as well as exaggeration of the day's events. We seem to need this

dream activity during our sleeping hours in order to preserve our personalities in an adjusted and healthy state. Ehrenwald suggests that people analogously need well-developed myths for this very same purpose in their waking
hours; if they are deprived of them, they will emit disturbed
behavior similar to that observed in individuals who have
been denied their ordinary pattern of dreaming. Man needs
this mythic kind of vision in order to keep himself together,
in order to maintain his adjustment, and to define himself accurately in space and time. Believing is a sensitive aspect of
human experience and myth is the extraordinary medium
through which man deals with the complexities of life and
incorporates them in an intelligible way into his own consciousness. Myth serves the believing person; it is not a romantic and irrelevant occurrence any more than dreaming
is. Man needs something more than hard facts and numbers
in order to understand his life. He cannot be real, in other
words, unless he has positive myths available to him; he
needs the language of myth to be able to believe; he needs
essential beliefs spoken in mythic language in order to live.

It is not surprising to find institutions, such as the organized Churches, somewhat hesitant to accept and incorporate
these new insights into the proclamation of old beliefs.
There is an inertia in all institutions that is quite natural.
They cannot be as responsive to changing situations as human beings, and it is a long and nearly miraculous process
when institutions can at last absorb and make use of what
the poets tell them about the world. That they manage to do
it at all is the extraordinary thing. That is why the Churches
have always needed prophets, perhaps beating their breasts
or speaking in a difficult language or behaving incompre-
hensibly as teachers, as processors of reality who attune the
Churches to the changing moods and needs of history. It is
not surprising that institutions, which seek necessarily to
maintain stability, hardly ever enthusiastically endorse new
developments either in theology or in science. They wait, as
time has taught them to, and often much longer than they

need to, before they open themselves in an unguarded way to new learning. The institutional Churches have always run the risk of making themselves unbelievable in the problems they have manifested in speaking about the nature of believing. In fact, many Churches have spoken in rather sure and absolute terms about this subject which cannot be discussed in this fashion very intelligibly at all. They have been quick to insist on their authority and their right to define and defend specific beliefs, but these stances have usually frustrated genuine religious searchers and moved genuine prophets to despair.

When an institution is sluggish, when authority shows little sign of being able to seek, in due time, for better constructs in which to speak about beliefs, then believers turn their gaze elsewhere for those who can speak to their experience and to their need to believe. An institution which has not completely lost its sensitivity to new language and new concepts is vital to the informed tasks of believing or of sharing beliefs with the men and women of its time. When institutions hold on to outmoded categories and symbols they cease speaking the language of believing altogether. And it is very hard for them to surrender these because, with their blind instincts, such institutions believe that they thereby surrender the faith itself. They have overidentified concrete ways of speaking of the faith with the idea of believing itself. It is this process, so endemic to institutions, that makes them seem perennially irrelevant to the world in which they live. When any Church shows signs of stirring, as the Roman Catholic Church did in Vatican Council II, the response to its efforts is enormous. When it slumps back, made fearful by its own initiatives, it causes the kind of disappointment that can only be known by people who truly want to believe and who sense that perhaps this institution, despite its encrustations, could still speak the vital words of life to all mankind. When you lose a feeling for the language of believing, you lose a sense of the dynamic meaning of believing.

One practical conclusion, of course, is not to make belief that sole possession of institutions, although institutions are obviously important for a community of believers. One must not expect institutions to surmount their inherent difficulties any more swiftly than any of us do. Perhaps we should learn to believe appropriately in institutions like the Church, not so much with a grain of salt as with a measure of compassion and understanding for the awkwardness and difficulty with which it must necessarily move through history. Indeed, the wonder is that it moves at all; believe in the institutional Church as it is, but that excludes instantaneous miracles from the organizational housing that can never quite catch up with the world around it. The danger with institutions is to overbelieve in them, to commit oneself beyond what is appropriate or even reasonable, in a blind and naïve loyalty that takes the name of faith even when it is only distantly related to it. Loyalty is not the same as faith, although a lot of ecclesiastics would like you to think so. We need a tolerant faith that the ecclesiastical institution will open itself more fully to its own poetic energies and be able to hear and speak the language of believing more clearly. Jesus told his disciples that they were called to speak "entirely new languages." The gift of tongues is not some mysterious, Berlitz-like capacity to speak German, French, and Arabic to various hearers, but to understand and to use effectively the language that speaks of believing in a truly human way. The institutional Churches have a struggle on their hands, but it is not to quell a riot or a rebellion, as it is popularly characterized and as some of its self-pitying leaders like to think. It is rather to become poetic again in giving men something to believe in.

Believing has also been observed in the medical and educational institutions of the world. It is no secret that faith that is alive, the activated capacity to believe in one's self and in one's future, is decisive for the health and growth of the person. This has been demonstrated many times in careful research on the role of believing in physical and psychological illness. Belief is at least as powerful as any medication known to man, but it is still one that is not understood very well. All we know, as psychiatrist Jerome B. Frank has told us in *Persuasion and Healing*,[3] is that there is a dynamic associated with believing in other persons that transforms their chances, reversing the odds in desperate situations and frequently making the difference between life and death. This has also been observed in education and in many other parts of life where the role of expectation—of an active optimistic belief in the potential of other individuals—has, in fact, enabled them to achieve performances beyond those that might on other grounds have been predicted for them. Believing is powerful medicine just as the failure to believe—the withholding of the investment of the self—is a negative and destructive force.

We may not be able to measure these transactions very well yet, but we can recognize them when they occur. When we do not believe in somebody, we have already taken away something of their chances for finding or becoming themselves. Teachers can do this to their students, coaches with their athletes, and priests to their people. Believing is not magic. It is profoundly human, a source of energy and self-integration, the like of which is not observed in any other aspect of human experience. In questions of growth, human relationships, and healthy achievement, the role of believing is crucial. It is faith, an active kind of believing, which makes men whole.

This opens to us the psychological world of believing, to the inner structures of personality which are so sensitive to its presence or its absence. In and with these structures the Spirit of Truth operates. Man may indeed be defined as a believing phenomenon, whose very life depends on finding the persons and the symbols through which he can understand and experience himself and his life fully. Believing is a social phenomenon and the person learns to believe best in a community of the faithful who provide the human setting

[3] Baltimore, Maryland: The Johns Hopkins Press, 1961.

for it. Believing is better than it is made to seem by institutional Churches which so slowly and cautiously expose themselves to new ideas about it; it is more lively than it seems in organizations so set on maintaining their own adjustment and stability that they ignore the unfolding dimensions of their opportunity or service to believing persons.

Believing is, then, central to understanding man, as vital to him as anything we know. The person believes with all of himself, and he recognizes and responds without effort to those who can speak faith's special language to him. We need to believe appropriately in the institutions that are meant to preserve and share the faith but not with the blind loyalty that kills believing altogether. Man just is not himself unless he believes and is believed in; that is the abiding wonder of living faith.

Chapter Three

INSIDE BELIEF

In a very real sense each of us men and women makes our own world. Not one of us is completely passive to any of the experiences we have in life. We actively fashion these, or we would be strangers to invention and learning as well as real love. Something of us has to get into these, or they would not exist at all. The role of the knower, the philosopher tells us, is crucial to the character of the knowledge he acquires. The inner states of the lover, as psychological research informs us, define the truth or falsity of the friendship in which he is a partner. The same reciprocal dynamic applies to the believer; he or she cannot be thought of as merely passive to the gift of faith; the person is, in fact, an integral part of the believing response itself. Without an understanding of the active role of the believer there can be no understanding of belief at all. An appreciation of believing demands a redefinition of faith as the living positive response of the believer; it is strongly dependent upon and conditioned by the believer's general psychological readiness for this. Faith does not float freely in an engulfing supernatural atmosphere; the human element is strongly determinative.

Faith is faulted hopelessly when it is conceived of in an extrinsic or static fashion. It is not a possession in the manner of an inert object which, no matter how much we cherish it, can never become a part of ourselves. Faith is not born outside of us nor does it take its strength and significance from a distant sphere that is defined over against human awareness and human experience. The charges that any view of faith that relates it too intimately to the personality of man is excessively naturalistic is indeed familiar. It echoes a divided model of the universe and of man which can no longer profitably be employed in discussing a subject as sensitive as religious faith and belief. To suggest that faith is generated in the heart of human personality and that it parallels its course of growth is to stand in true wonder at God's grandeur.

The effort to make faith some kind of objective entity, capriciously given or withheld and haphazardly earned or lost, has made it more rather than less difficult to understand the believing nature of man. Living faith can only be seen in living persons; it demands that we observe the slow and humanly conditioned process through which our capacity to believe is activated. Believing is influenced, as is our perception of the world, by our inner states in relationship to external sources of stimulation.

Many factors combine their influence in forming the texture of this faith-perception of the universe. A close look at man shows that faith is not a simple notion, like the image of the totally natural man flooded by rays of grace coming down from heaven. Indeed, as we proceed in our understanding of faith, we enter into depths of human individuality previously untapped and frequently unrecognized. There is, in other words, a non-rational dimension to the faith response which radiates from layers of human experience to which rational language is a stranger. These dynamic facets of personality are powerfully influential in shaping our understanding of our world; and in and through them we learn meanings of life that we never quite get into words but nonetheless know. At this level of human experience we appreciate the need for myths and symbols as an ancient but always fresh and necessary language of human personality. Faith lives at this level in each one of us.

As we have retired the model of a divided universe with the advent of the age of science and space flight, so too we have been forced to put aside the models of divided man which were necessary to sustain older concepts of faith as static and separate from ourselves and our own human unity. Faith is closely linked to man, a living quality as pervasive and real as his spirit and similarly related to his total identity. There is no believing that does not involve the whole man. You cannot give the response of faith with only a part of your personality. This would be to contradict and to diminish the fullness of the stance we are required to take through any profession of personal faith. Faith comes from the whole of us, or it is hardly faith. Believing has rational elements, of course, but its roots run through our sinews and unconscious pathways, through all the aspects of our personality, in other words, to which insufficient attention has previously been paid. This has not necessarily been a difficulty for the common person who, unhobbled by excessively rational analysis or self-consciousness, has often felt belief as a deep and organizing part of himself, something of the heart as well as the mind. That is why people have always responded to effective symbols of belief—because they could understand and respond to that language even if they could not parse it.

Faith involves struggle, an effort to sense the fullness of ourselves at the moment we commit ourselves in belief. And to believe is essential to the activation and co-ordination of all the processes through which we reach toward our own individuality and fullness. Believing is related to the complex human process we call growth; its character is keyed to the total development of ourselves.

There is something fundamental about believing that transcends any specific categories of creed or other intellectual statements of beliefs. It is, as growth is more than rational statements concerning life, much more than that. This root quality of believing concerns us in this chapter. As Paul Tillich has observed, "Faith in the biblical view, is an act of the whole personality. Will, knowledge, and emotion participate in it. It is an act of self-surrender, of obedience, of assent. Each of these elements must be present."[1] Believing

[1] *Biblical Wisdom and the Search for Ultimate Reality* (Chicago: University of Chicago Press, 1955), p. 53.

cannot, then, be separated from the personality of the believer. To believe fully is proof that we are there, that the elements of our identity cohere, that we have a sense of ourselves we can invest in something outside of ourselves. I believe, we might say, therefore, I am. The act of believing brings us altogether.

So too believing is subject to the approximately understood laws of development that regulate all the other aspects of human growth. Believing does not live above and beyond the growing personality; it does not possess a fully mature mode of being independent of the individual's general personal development. Believing is a positive capacity that is fed by and, like a river gathering strength from collateral streams, feeds human experience. It is born in it and comes to be able to give it shape; it does not, however, exist without it. Faith is so tied up with our growing that it is notably affected, from infancy onward, by the relationships that are significant in the individual's life. This environment of human beings is exactly right to actuate all our capacities, including that of believing.

In the development of faith we note the gathering together of some of the most basic and prized signatures of human experience. These include, as Professor Thomas A. Droege has observed,[2] trust, obedience, knowledge, assent, commitment and centeredness. All these ultimately demand an investment of the whole person. As the individual man or woman grows, the meaning and quality of these experiences shift, and one may become more important than the other; although never totally independent of each other, they may be stressed differently at various points on the curve of development.

The origins of our capacity to believe lie in our earliest experience when, in helplessness and without words, we begin to sense the world as believable or not. We possess the latent possibilities of believing, but whether and to what ex-

[2] "Developmental View of Faith," *Journal of Religion and Health*, Vol. 11, No. 4, October 1972, p. 314.

tent we exercise these depends on the reactions of those persons closest to us. We should not, of course, be surprised by the idea of faith as a component of personality shaped by interpersonal experience. Jesus seems to speak of it this way in the Gospels, pointing to little children for an understanding of the meaning of believing. He did not mean merely to underscore them as models of trust and openness; sometimes children are not like that at all. Instead, Jesus' comparison suggests also the human context in which children grow and develop into mature believers. This movement depends on the manner in which their beginning faith is greeted by the believers who bring them up. The quality of believing that we experience from others in our earliest development is a crucial determinant of the style of belief of which we are then capable. Whether we believe hinges on whether we are believed in. It is interesting to recall the nature of the authority parents exercise over children. It springs from their relationship, because they are the authors of the children, and not from some extrinsic set of rules. It is a relationship that takes on its meaning from the special relationship of the human beings involved in it. This is a totally different order of experience from that of politics, manipulation, or impersonal power. The existence and health of parental authority depends on their capacity to stay in relationship—and to change the relationship appropriately—with their growing children. This kind of authority speaks to us of the original meaning of the word: to make able to grow. The development of faith falls into this order of experience too. It is calibrated to interpersonal realities, to those near mysterious transactions between people that cannot be faked and that cannot be claimed to exist when, in fact, they do not. Faith depends on a reality like friendship rather than a rule of law. As a human capacity it is energized only by other humans who actually believe in us.

This makes it all the more regrettable that faith has been treated as something responsive to the commands of power by some ecclesiastics. Faith has never grown because of force or manipulation; genuine faith has, in fact, always been stronger than these exercises of power. It is obviously not very helpful to instruct people in belief through threats of present or imminent punishments. People may well give some kind of assent to religious formulas under this pressure but it is never true faith. In the same way, it is obvious that those persons who help people to find or to rediscover their faith are profoundly human believers themselves. Pope John XXIII is a well-known example of this, a believing pastor whose authority lay not in power but in love. He made believing easier for human beings.

It is proper to ask, in this context, whether we can find any difference, or whether we should presume that any would exist, in the basic character of our believing response toward God and toward each other. It is difficult to imagine that some other activity, alien but superior to our human belief capacity, is required in order to have faith in God. Once again the statements of Jesus are instructive. His invitation is to "believe in me," a statement that cannot possibly be grasped by anyone who does not know something about friendship and love. Faith language is human language, after all, and if friendship with God does not have a human face then it is beyond us completely. We return to man to understand anything and everything about faith in God. This is the message and the incarnation, but in a world where some theologies still insist on a kind of dread or a terror before the awesome face of God, we may forget that believing is a human activity, part of what God gave us to respond to each other and to Him. We believe best, not when we escape our human condition, but when we are at ease and untroubled about it. Openness to God is mediated always by our human condition. Faith is a living filament threaded through all our existence, and as we trace this through the personal relationships through which we have learned to believe, we join ourselves to the mystery of believing in someone beyond us.

It is unfortunately true that the institutional concern for

orthodoxy, as sociologist of religion Robert Bellah has observed, has often been more properly a concern to maintain religious authority. When this authority is not conceived of as a living experience, it cannot vitalize faith,
although it may fix it in static statements of belief and create
an illusion of security. Believing in any human context never
deepens merely because of security. Believing lives in a
more perilous and contingent world, not in some double-
guarded ecclesiastical Fort Knox. Faith, in fact, is uneasy
with too much security; what, indeed, could faith mean in
a totally predictable world? Churchmen who worry too
much about the loss of faith may never have learned to believe themselves. It is not an exaggeration to suggest that
many prelates who seem quite anxious about what others believe in do not seem to believe much in their people. So, too,
contemporary parents who are excessively upset about their
children's attitude toward religion may be telling us about
their own shaky faith. They find it difficult to communicate
faith because they conceive of it too exclusively in terms of
duty rather than as a living testimony to God's existence and
goodness to us. Religion is always given a bad name, and
faith seems like a soggy burden when it is urged by people
who do not believe fundamentally in the capacity of other
people at all. These people shield themselves from others
and thus make themselves unbelievable. Nothing is emptier
than sermons on faith in God preached by clergy who cannot believe in persons. Unbelieving ritual gestures made in
the name of such faith are probably the most obscene gestures in the history of the world.

The infant's fundamental faith-shaping experience is associated with developing a sense of trust, that is a perception of the world as a friendly and reliable place in
which people intend to do him good rather than harm. This,
according to psychoanalyst Erik Erikson, is the work of the
first year of life and the responsibility and opportunity of
the mother. It is not surprising that something so intimate
and human should be the scene of our first trembling ex-

perience of the meaning of trust, a variable that is closely
related to our unfolding ability to believe in the world and
in others around us. What begins with another person
grows in a social or community setting. That is one of the
best arguments for an organized Church; it is meant to be
an assemblage of people, a believing community that
stands around us at our baptism to affirm us and to provide
the environment of interpersonal support in which our capacity to believe is differentiated and strengthened.

Perhaps the ancient title Mother Church is not just accidental or merely a sentimental statement after all. It
catches the essential responsive quality of the Christian community as the continuing environment for our development in faith. It is a nurturing community concerned with
our growing toward a mature position within it. This is a
very different feeling from a Church that sees baptism as
largely ceremonial and unrelated, in any way that makes
a difference, to a growing reality known as faith. No one,
as the tradition of the Church attests, expects the infant
child to possess fully developed faith. The whole practice
of the Church has always acknowledged this. Faith grows
in the context of relationship to adult believers. When the
Church senses itself as a living mystery, as a people rather
than a bureaucracy, then it becomes an authentic mystical
and transforming presence in the world. That is what is
meant by a faith community, a gathering of believers who
understand faith in terms other than submission; it may not
be able to put this into words and so it returns to the fundamental language of the Spirit, that of myth and symbol.
When faith is merely imposed and can easily be perceived
as impersonal and demanding, it is a shell that does not
touch or express human experience or longing. Only a living
faith can be spoken of in symbols like the kingdom and the
treasure. If faith is inconsistent or spotty and shallow in
places it cripples rather than enlarges the growing person's
capacity to trust or believe. Inconsistency of response has
frequently been highlighted as destructive of the growth

of moral character.[3] Inconsistency rather than heresy is the greatest enemy of developing faith. And inconsistency is the contribution of those who are estranged from the human foundations of believing.

Believing as conditioned by initial trust is not an invitation to gullibility or to inappropriate innocence. As Erikson and other observers have pointed out, the developing person must learn to mistrust as well as to trust other persons and events. This is a subtle but significant aspect of believing which is dependent on our overall development as persons. We cannot enter a difficult world without a certain measure of sensitivity to its evils and its deceptions. An undifferentiated and naïve response to everything around us quickly destroys us and cuts off further growth. Part of the process of learning to believe lies in being able to tell the difference between something or someone that is believable and something that is not. This is a healthy response that pays tribute to the depth and complexity of human personality; it introduces us to a world in which evil exists in ourselves and in others. The believer has to live in that contingent world, and he cannot survive if he is inappropriately innocent.

Faith, as has been mentioned before, focuses for us some of our most essential life experiences, awarenesses that continue to develop and that eventually become signs of whether we have achieved a fullness of our humanity or not. These are the experiences that take us out of the shallows of existence and into the depths where we begin to comprehend everything that is painfully beautiful and occasionally terrifying about the world and other persons. It is in this world that we believe, a difficult and sometimes hostile place where we will not survive in a very healthy condition without a finely attuned sense of what it means to believe. Believing is risky not because it invites us into the unknown but because it requires us constantly to con-

[3] Peck, Robert; and Havighurst, Robert, *The Psychology of Moral Development* (New York: John Wiley & Sons, 1962).

front what we actually do know about the world, that it is a place where we may be hurt, or misunderstood, or left alone in sickness or in the grip of some other large or small defeat. Faith leads us deeper into reality; it makes living in the real world possible. Faith untempered by a sense of all that is still incomplete about us and human affairs is still in its infancy.

To return to the relational context of believing, it is clear that faith incorporates us into the mystery of revelation. Believing and revelation are almost two sides of the same experience. The impulse to believe, to form constructs about the world and our destiny, makes us aware gradually of ourselves. So too, as we make our grasp on this revelation of ourselves more sure, we are freer to reveal ourselves to others, to communicate the truth of our personalities to them, and to commit ourselves to them in a personal manner. This dynamic process is fired by the faith that opens us to the revelation others make of themselves to us. Believing leads to mutual revelation, and the light of this revelation makes clear the way to deeper and firmer belief. This is a reciprocal process that marks all our days when we are alive to each other; it also enables us to have some insight into the God who reveals himself and makes himself believable in our human condition.

Faith calls forth a response that is as complete a gift of ourselves as possible. Living faith is of the entire man, as has been observed, rather than merely of his intellect or of his emotions. It is something that we experience well only when we are living in a relatively well-integrated fashion. Faith, as the Gospels tell us, makes us whole, not in some pleasant descriptive sense, but because it draws forth the fullness of ourselves and the truth of our own personalities. There is no way to believe except through our own identities. This cannot be a half-measure thing or an activity that can be engaged in while we are really thinking of something else. Simply said, we must be all there to each other and to God to be believers. When there is a defect in this total response fidelity is imperiled. The collapse of believing occurs when what we believe is really divorced from the way we live. That is to say, we stop believing when we hold back from life and from each other. This is true in marriage and friendship, and it is also true in any other kind of response that pivots on a genuine investment of ourselves. Instead of believing we are often thinking about believing; we make a check mark on some creed as a security measure, but we are actually blinding ourselves to the full measure of religious reality when we take this restricted view. We are taking ourselves out of the environment where faith lives, and we numb ourselves to the authentic religious experience of our lives.

Faith is, therefore, not merely intellectual, and obedience to authority cannot consist only in accepting certain statements about faith. The obediential element is surely present in believing but, again, this is far more as it is found in friendship and love, the analogies that Jesus himself persisted in using to describe his Kingdom against the authoritarian churchman of his own day. The obedience of faith, like that of friends to each other, asks us to listen to and respond to the depths of our honest experience, to what, when we are open and true, we recognize as taking place in and between ourselves and others. It is obedience to the truth of ourselves and our lives that is the essential psychological note of the true believer.

Faith orients us to greater life, to bringing more of ourselves and of others alive than before we began to believe. Through faith we become more present to ourselves, to our neighbor, and to God. Through faith we continue to grow in these relationships, sensing more deeply as time passes how they encompass and reflect the essential religious themes of the Gospel, meeting and loving, dying and rising, waiting and being filled. We learn the profound and mystical language of believing, recognizing God's truths for us in the thousand glimpses we get of him in the activities and aspirations of everyday life. Believing breaks us open to the revelation that innervates the life of the Spirit. The Church provides and celebrates the human sharing that is the source of our development until we are strong enough to give of our faith to make others whole.

Chapter Four

INCARNATIONAL FAITH

We all know the experience of suddenly seeing something with which we are familiar in a new way or in a fresh light. It can be something as simple as the sunrise, an old friend, or some truth about ourselves. We say spontaneously that this "is like seeing it for the first time." We have also known those moments of insight when we could suddenly identify, through the words or symbols of another, a profound truth of our own experience. We say, for example, "That makes sense of the way I have felt." Or, in a slightly different vein, "That's the way I have felt about it for a long while, but I never understood it until now." These human discoveries are only a small portion of the bulky catalogue of surprises that fill a growing life.

Other aspects of ourselves and our world exist and cannot easily be seen in fresh perspective. We have stabilized convictions or ideas about ourselves and others that we do not really examine because we feel we know just about everything about these subjects. Our religious faith is one of these dimensions of experience we sometimes never hold up to the light for a fresh examination. Yet faith as a living part of our personalities is constantly changing whether we notice it or not. We have to search for the right light of honesty in which to view it as a growing part of ourselves.

The Second Vatican Council held faith up to the light in an extraordinarily human and sensitive manner. Through their reflections, the bishops of the world have made it possible for us to look freshly at something we had considered as resistant to change as the rock of ages. Faith has thus become a more exciting and relevant subject as it is perceived in relationship to the great struggles of mankind for individual and social development. We are familiar with the outdated static concept of faith, a notion that lingers mostly as a memory. It is necessary briefly to recall this, however, in order to walk slowly around the vital concept of faith which now stands as the dynamic achievement of the understanding of modern theology and pastoral reflection.

Faith was once conceived of as opening us to a world we could not otherwise see; it alerted us to a coexistent spiritual world that hovered somewhere just above this one like a tide of pure white clouds that would one day wash the earth free of its grime. Faith elevated us and, in a sense, rescued us from all that was purely natural; it enabled us to affirm what was not immediately visible, the realm of spiritual reality that was conceived of as distinct from and superior to the order of our general human experience. This faith was something for which we could pray although it was something we could never merit; it demanded a surrender of the self, and as a powerful way of structuring our inner and outer worlds, it had enormous practical consequences on the way we conducted our lives. This faith was important because its possession determined our salvation. The Church's concern about this style of faith led it on occasions to be quite insensitive in its dealings with the customs, feelings, and world views of those peoples to whom the Gospel was to be preached by bands of heroic missioners. They were pagans, unbelievers, the spiritually unwashed, who had to be invested at all costs with saving faith.

Some old applications of this medallionlike faith not only turned men away from what was natural but also devalued the very concept of the natural, perceiving man's inner states as flawed with inadmissible desires and tendencies. These latter included what we now recognize as some of his healthy aspirations as well as his emotional life which, according to this former outlook, had to be tightly supervised and controlled. A shorthand view of the kind of faith that was passed on to the average person was buttressed by the assurances of authority. This style of belief was demanding in one way but a sure thing for salvation in another. Some of the principal stresses of this rather elementary notion of faith—which in an oversimplified version prevailed in many ordinary peoples' lives—were those in which faith was tested by a struggle which generally pitted the inner spiritual man against the outer fleshly man. The just man, according to the Scriptures, lived by faith, but in this version, he did it through maintaining a basic antagonism with his own personality. The articles of practical faith which received paramount moral emphasis centered on man's sexual understanding and behavior. Indeed, in the view of many ecclesiastics, these still constitute the test of the faithful person.

This manner of looking at the world and themselves led people to experience tension between the spirit and the flesh as well as between anything that was proud and stubborn in themselves and everything that was lofty and redemptive in the spiritual sphere. This faith urged them to give up themselves, their ambitions, and the world itself. This promoted a functional estrangement of man from himself. This is familiar material, of course, but people continue to reflect and talk about it precisely because the imprint of this faith on their own self-awareness has been so profound and, in many cases, so hurting as well. The spite of rueful Catholic nostalgia books attests to that. Faith possessed a quality of demand but little of celebration. It is not surprising that many people became confused or angered at a faith that imposed a meaning on themselves and their lives that did not seem to match their own experience. That this type of faith offered meaning and achieved results is undeniable.

We must now investigate what happens to our self-understanding when we get a sudden new perspective on faith. This new angle of vision on faith may generate that sense of surprise and elation that accompanies our recognition of an understanding that has been forming inside of us for a long time.

If faith is something that can be separated neither from personality nor from life, then the previous tendency to find its tests in the antagonism between the spirit and the flesh, or between the pride of intellect and the grace of obedience, must be reinspected. The eyes of faith do not, in fact, focus always on another world that is totally beyond and different from this one in character and expectations. To recognize believing as much a part of us as our breath means that the eyes of faith allow us to see more clearly man and his never-ending efforts to understand himself and his destiny. Faith that is incarnational enables us to see more and to do it from the vantage point of our earthly journey. This is precisely the shift of viewpoint that has been offered to us through the rediscovery of living faith by modern theology.

The New Testament message emphasizes that God so loved the world that he sent his only begotten son to it. The Father has chosen to reveal himself, not in an invisible way, but through a faith made concrete in the humanity of Jesus. Jesus as Lord comes to show us how to live life rather than how to escape it; he spares himself nothing of human experience except sin and, in a way that reveals the mythic language of faith very clearly, speaks in parables and stories through which we can recognize the stories of our own lives. Jesus asks for belief in himself, a human transaction dependent upon our willingness to grow as fully as possible in our efforts to respond to him. Jesus compares the mystery of his relationship to the Church with the human relationship between bride and groom. There is nothing in his preaching or in his life that suggests that the reality of faith precludes the hard but joyful realities of this life which we share with each other. Faith that is centered in this life, that understands itself as proclaiming the kingdom which is in our very midst, awakens us to a sense of ourselves as living in and by the Spirit that has been given to us. In other words, the incarnational faith preached by Jesus enables us to understand our lives and, far from estranging us from our inner states, makes it possible for us to identify the yearnings, conflicts, and other important aspects of our experience together as essentially sacred. Incarnational belief opens us, of course, to a meaning larger than our own small lives, but it does this through helping us look more deeply into rather than away from ourselves.

This is the restored sense of faith which has emerged from Vatican Council II. It is of such faith that the remarkable document on *The Church in the Modern World* speaks its most eloquent phrases. Indeed, it is through a recognition of the intimately human nature of our faith response, that the Council proclaims clearly the necessary conditions of freedom and respect which must surround an individual's affirmation of his own religious belief. A recent popularized description of faith catches these notes quite well.[1] "Christian faith is a claim to an accurate understanding of this world, human existence and the gracious Being of God; an understanding which is given in the being, life, actions and teachings of Jesus Christ; and one which calls for and makes possible the humanization of men and the worship of God the Father, in a community witnessing to the presence of His Kingdom on earth."

Faith gives us a way of understanding this world in Jesus; incarnational faith awakens us to life in all its dimensions and enables us to see how religious reality is interwoven with our own experience. Far from being separate and distinct, something to which we can only aspire if we empty ourselves of our human cares and yearning, faith reveals itself as necessarily connected with the personal growth and development of men and women. The seeds of faith are sown deeply in human personality, and they do not contradict although they are conditioned by man's na-

[1] Daniel O'Dugan, *Faith for Tomorrow* (Dayton: Pflaum Press, 1969), p. 43.

ture and by the formational psychological experiences through which he achieves his own unique character.

Such faith is geared to growth. It lights up the meaning of this world, allowing us to see the pathway we must follow if, individually or collectively, we are to achieve our destiny as God's children. To become fully human becomes the task of the religious person. This is the first response of believing that men and women have possibilities, that our faith must be concerned with these or we will never discover or understand ourselves. If faith did not allow us to believe in this world and in each other, then we would all be better off quitting it for the mountains and the monasteries, abandoning it to its misery and final apocalyptic death throes. This has never, however, been the tone nor the fundamental intuition of Christianity. The Gospels, and the Church's teaching of them, even when it was confused about their literal meaning, has always been concerned with man and his meaning. It is difficult to speak about self-fulfillment in an age in which movements aimed at actualizing human potential are so numerous and are frequently characterized by shallowness of concept and operation. Self-fulfillment has come to sound like some kind of selfish joy ride which concerns itself with sensual pleasure more than spiritual reality. But fulfillment is a fair enough name for what the Christian seeks for himself and others when he lives by faith.

At the heart of it, incarnational faith opens men and women to life and to what it means if we have a personal belief in Jesus. This necessarily turns us back to experiencing and expressing incarnational faith at the numerous crossroads of choice and meaning that dot the path of our development. This struggle to respond to our fundamental human challenges involves us in a dying and rising that recur, like the theme of a great symphony, as the resonations of our faith life in Jesus. A deep faith opens us to the essential Gospel experience: anyone who tries to love necessarily recreates and re-experiences the incarnational rhythm of the life of Jesus. Faith recognizes the patterns of birth, death, and resurrection which are in every life as the experiences through which we know the mystery and meaning of our existence.

Incarnational faith is connected with a progressive and ever-finer self-definition. As has been mentioned before, faith as revelation initiates an awareness of our true selves and the nature of our relationships with each other. Faith is concerned with ourselves and others; its test, far from being limited to certain aspects of our behavior, such as the sexual, centers on everything about us when we stand face to face, at all the levels of our being, with each other. Incarnational faith, by its very nature, is never perfectly or fully developed. As we strive to respond, it opens us further, helping us, at levels where words may not yet be available to us, to grasp some of our own significance and to sense our participation in the meaning of the world. Through this faith we understand the continuity between our human experience and our ultimate fulfillment in God. There is nothing that God asks of us that contradicts or destroys anything that is healthy about our humanity. Only such a faith can illumine the growth of marriage, the mystery of creativity, or the wonder of our differences.

It is obvious that the faith which successfully interprets and sustains the meaning of human experience has powerful effects on those who affirm it. This has been true of deeply held beliefs all through the course of history. It also explains man's yearning to believe, and sometimes his willingness to believe in outlandish things and individuals when he is denied richer and fuller explanations of his own existence. Belief that matches our urge to grow not only confers a sense of significance on us but it also gives us a sense of direction. That is why Jesus says, "I am the way." Faith in him does not move us to look at man and see less; it urges us to see more by pressing us to come to terms with everything that is part of us. Faith allows us a better sense of ourselves and moves us toward more honest self-understanding, making us face the evil as well as the good that lies within ourselves. Only as we understand the elements of our personality can we forge the identity that best expresses our human individuality. Believing is very closely tied up with this identification process which never goes on outside of it. Incarnational belief, in other words, does not operate in a vacuum or as though man and his culture had no effect on the possible development of belief itself.

Anyone who is conversant with the psychological and sociological research on the nature of religious belief will admit that although the measures and modes of its expression are still in need of greater refinement, they catch some of the dynamic of incarnational faith. It has been suggested by Thomas Droege that faith develops in accord with the major growth challenges of the individual man or woman. Only the approach to faith that flows from this central notion of growth offers the possibility of integrating the wide range of human experiences that eventually shape us and our way of believing. These begin, as has been mentioned earlier, with the basic and unconscious experience of trust during the first months of life. This sharply conditions, for good or for evil, the child's sense of expectation toward the world as a friendly and dependable place. The individual who does not experience adequate trust at this stage may spend the rest of his life searching for it and may, in fact, find that it is always difficult for him to profess an act of faith in other persons or institutions. Denied the impact of a trustworthy environment, an individual begins life with a major handicap in developing his faith response. This is not to say that later relationships cannot help the individual greatly in understanding and experiencing the meaning of faith, although such happy endings cannot be counted upon. The child who is not believed in will find it difficult to believe in himself or in the world in which he must grow and live.

So, too, in developmental process, the child must achieve a sense of autonomy. Without this, the individual cannot come to a sense of his own separateness or define himself in terms of his own will. The struggle for autonomy is the struggle for healthy independence, and this is also strongly conditioned by the human relationships that surround a person at this point in life. As Droege observes,[2] "The infant's basic faith in existence, which is the lasting treasure saved from the first developmental stage, must not be jeopardized by the sudden violent wish to have a choice." It is a time of struggle and conflict within as well as outside the individual. This move toward a sense of the self is just as important in moving toward adult faith as it is in the general process of growing up. The individual who is not independent, who cannot choose for himself, has difficulty in sorting himself out from his own experiences. As the individual moves into the world of reality, as he finds that he must define his autonomy in terms of persons who are separate from himself and who also possess rights distinct from his own, a major step is made toward the awareness of self that is an integral part of faith at the more mature level of existence.

The next challenge of faith parallels the individual's adolescent task of coming to terms with himself and of investing himself in commitments of one kind or another. The well-publicized adolescent search for identity finds the young person dealing with the factors that must be understood if he or she is to draw close to another in intimacy. The principal challenge is concerned with the meaning of fidelity, with the individual's capacity to give himself steadily to another person or to a cause. Only when he or she masters this can they possess their identity as believable and believing individuals who can move in and through the lives of others under their own psychological power. There is no way an individual can commit himself if he lacks this sense of who he is and how he differs from others; he simply will have nothing with which to relate to others. This achievement of identity is a necessary foundation for any adult

[2] Op. cit., p. 323.

belief or relationship to God Himself. While these reflections on the overall process of human growth are necessarily abbreviated for this discussion, it is still easy to see how these various works of development are essential to the full-bodied act of faith we expect to find in adults. This kind of believing does not arrive full blown or independent of the people and processes through which an authentic sense of the self and its capacity for commitment is derived. Faith is the kind of thing we learn as we learn to become ourselves.

Faith runs through the personality as the bloodstream does through the body; it not only gives life to the person but it is also affected notably by the overall health of the individual. Man, the perennial believer, simply cannot be divided up according to the fashion that allowed us once to speak of faith as a restricted operation touching man's intellect or will. Faith is more pervasive than that and must be considered in relationship to the total presence of an individual in life. To oversimplify for the moment, the less a person grows to his own individuality the more hampered he will be in developing his religious faith. On the other hand, the more fully human a person becomes, the more capable he is of exercising a vibrant, searching, and satisfying religious faith. Religion has suffered a twin kind of difficulty for many generations. Viewed by social scientists and medical specialists, it has often seemed a neurotic disorder, the manifestation of the search for magical solutions to life's difficulties, or the gropings of persons who have never satisfactorily resolved relationship to their parents. That is the kind of religion that can rightly be classed as the opium of the people. On the other hand, ascetic theologians have been as unkind to religion in quite another way. They heavily mortgaged it, making its highest expressions and experience the property of persons who seemed to disown or detach themselves thoroughly from their own human experience. Mysticism became the function of the well-keened psyche, the final triumph of the person who had vanquished the body in the name of spiritual glory.

Both of these views have made it difficult to look at religious faith as an aspect of the normal healthy personality. The research that has been prompted by the theoretical work of the late Gordon Allport over the last generation has done much to restore a sense of balance about the place of religion in life. No longer need it be conceived of, in its highest form, as the exclusive property of over-spiritualized mystics.

Allport suggested that religious faith could be conceived of on a continuum, the poles of which could be labeled intrinsic and extrinsic. Allport distinguished between these contents by identifying intrinsic religion as a master motive through which an individual is able to organize and understand all the experiences of his life. Intrinsic faith, in Allport's view, is a well-developed and mature kind of religious belief. On the other hand, however, extrinsic religion represents the compartmentalized and quite external form of religious behavior which has no roots in the individual's personality. Far from being that through which the person is able to judge his actions and guide his life, extrinsic religion is a utilitarian and instrumental phenomenon which he uses to fulfill obligations, allay fears, and to hold on to for the sake of his own salvation. This is the religion of the immature or underdeveloped person whose other outlooks and convictions parallel the shallow quality of his religious orientation. In further research, for example, Allport sought to demonstrate that racial prejudice was frequently found among people who could be described as extrinsically religious; it was not found in subjects judged to possess a more mature religious outlook.

Essentially, extrinsic religion represents a non-integrated value, the significance of which is grasped only superficially and the effects of which are found minimally in the way a person directs his life. It is closely akin to the religion of childhood, an unquestioned inheritance which is accepted on the authority of those who instruct the individual in its tenets. It never moves much beyond this in the life of the extrinsically religious person. The maturely religious person, however, passes through a crisis of belief in which he questions what he has received from others in order to test it against what he has learned from his own experience. Some persons abandon religious convictions of a formal sort at this time of crisis in their lives, sometimes because the fundamentalistic beliefs in which they were reared no longer seem adequate to explain the universe or their knowledge of it. Others turn back from the crisis to hold onto the faith which seems endangered by previously unthinkable questions. The growing person, however, accepts the challenge of self-examination and transforms his faith through a process of internalization at this stage of life. Now he believes for himself rather than on the authority of someone else. The outcome of developed religious faith is quite parallel, in Allport's design, to the self-responsible characteristics of the mature individual who judges his own experience in the light of the evidence he is able to procure for himself.

This conceptualization of religious faith enables us to understand it as a developmental problem. As such, it is no different from any other developmental problem of human beings. They can, after all, be challenged by crises for which they are not prepared; their general development can be arrested by a complex of social forces and pressures; they can advance into the mature years of life with the psychological equipment of an adolescent. One must look beneath the appearance in order to discover the true psychological state of the individual within. Religious faith seems to be correlated with the other developmental processes; it does not operate independent of them. Although Allport's schema has been subjected to an array of technical and theoretical criticism, it has proved durable and, in the words of Yale Professor James E. Dittes, it shows a considerable promise of surviving its obituary. Most of the research that has employed the intrinsic-extrinsic paradigm has tended to support Allport's general outlook. Indeed, a recent survey of the priests of the United States, conducted through the psychological department of Loyola University of Chicago, addressed itself, in part, to the quality of faith of the subjects of the investigation. The results of this study demonstrate the richness of Allport's conceptualization as well as the developmental nature of religious faith.

In conjunction with the other instruments and extensive interviews carried out during the pilot projects and actual study, a special maturity of faith scale was developed that enabled the researchers to make judgments on whether the developmental level of the faith of the respondents reflected their overall personal development. The main body of the research made it possible to assign American priests to various categories reflecting the stage of their psychological development. These were labeled the *maldeveloped,* the *underdeveloped,* the *developing,* and the *developed.* In the maldeveloped category are those persons who, although still functioning in the priesthood, give evidence of serious and chronic psychological problems that have interfered in a marked way with their personal and professional lives. The underdeveloped do not manifest such serious difficulties; rather, they reflect a failure or inability to come to terms with the adult challenges of psychological growth. They are considered underdeveloped in that their psychological age does not match their chronological age. Although they look adult, and have adult responsibilities, these men have generally failed to resolve the tasks a man must face in the adolescent stage in his life. The developing group comprise individuals who, although they had been arrested in their growth for a time, have begun to grow again and to deal with the unfinished business of their personal development. There is much energy in this group, a clearly dynamic cluster of individuals for whom the pursuit of unfinished growth became the most important business of their lives. The developed group of priests represents the individuals who have dealt successfully with the various stages of their lives, have developed their capacities well, and who, although not absolutely perfect, represent what we understand by psychological health.

In those aspects of the research which investigated religious faith, it is fascinating to observe the gradations of faith that seem to follow closely on the subjects' levels of personal development. The *maldeveloped* show the greatest number of characteristics of extrinsic faith. The *underdeveloped*, while more advanced than the *maldeveloped*, still evidence more signs of extrinsic faith than either the *developed* or *developing* groups. Interestingly enough, the priests in the *developing* group manifest a slightly higher index of intrinsic religious faith factors than do those in the *developed* group. All of the groups, however, are more intrinsic in their religious faith, in a statistically significant way, than the *maldeveloped* group of subjects.

Why would the *developing* group seem at least equal to the *developed* group in the nature of their intrinsic religious faith? The answer is probably connected with the fact that they are more vitally involved in dealing with their psychological growth, more excited about it, than any of the other groups in the study. While relatively complete integration of personality is obviously a desired stage of development, the rediscovery and pursuit of this seems to activate a person's energies in a quite remarkable way. This is also evidenced on another psychological test, the Personal Orientation Inventory, on which the developing group scored more highly than any of the other groups. To come psychologically alive is a process that has profound effects on all of a person's behavior. It seems, in other words, that when a person shakes off the lethargy of arrested personal development the intensity of the experience is reflected in some way in everything he does, including the way he scores on psychological tests. There is an exuberance which reflects the dynamic of growth that has been re-engaged. It is not surprising to find individuals who could be classified as *developing* slightly more intrinsic in their orientation than even the *developed*. They are presenting themselves with questions for which they previously thought they had the answers and they are, in some sense, enjoying the ambiguity of the experience. It is still difficult for them to test the nature of their religious faith and to peer into their own psychological adjustment, especially if this has been embarrassingly preadolescent. There is, however, a remarkable positive trust in human persons through which they move themselves forward when they have at last come in contact with the real heart of their own life experience. There is an overflow, a sense of feeling alive, that accompanies discovery of new depths both in oneself and in one's faith. The data of this study support the general concept that the quality of an individual's religious faith is inseparably related to the level of his psychological development. Faith does not stand alone, nor outside the personality; it is something we understand only if we understand the persons who exercise it.

Several questions arise in the light of these findings. First of all, one can lay aside the contention that religious faith is merely a neurotic outcropping. It is clear that the deepest and most functional religious faith is a property of the individual who has the best sense of himself, his own powers, and his purpose in life. People who believe maturely also relate to themselves and to their neighbors maturely. They have dealt with the questions of life that mark man off as separate from the other orders of creation. With authentic awareness they have learned some of the lessons of loving, the highest expression of which has always been conceded to represent the highest operational definition of religious faith. This is not to deny that neurotic religion can exist; it manifestly does in the lives of many persons whose needs give shape to the world they inhabit. Their faith generally reflects something about their overall adjustment: As a man is, so he seems to believe. There is nothing startling in this, although it is refreshing to find evidence to support it. Secondly, mysticism cannot be the exclusive property of people who, in some arduous fashion, have overcome the body in order to live almost exclusively the life of the spirit. This is to make the richest expression of religious faith a function of the disintegrated personality. We may have to look much more carefully at our discussions of psychological adjustment, and it is difficult to imagine that they should be absent in the life of a person who lives by a deep and lively faith. What is truly mystical may, in other words, be present in the intensity of life of persons who are psychologically well adjusted. They are able to love and trust others deeply; they have a sense of possession of themselves and a capacity for entering into life in a profound way. Mysticism may be made up of such experiences rather than of the extraordinary and sometimes seemingly bizarre behaviors with which it has often been described. Mysticism, in other words, is found in the heart of human experience rather than at its remote and inaccessible edges. Perhaps we have overlooked the healthy kind of adjustment that seems to be present in the lives of great figures, such as Teresa of Avila, and distorted what seems to be other than this. Many people resist this interpretation of profound religious behavior, finding it too prosaic and too unromantic. Nonetheless, if religious and healthy personal growth go hand in hand, then we must put mysticism back into a more realistic psychological perspective.

Thirdly, it is clear that the unity of human experience is attested to by both Allport's theory and the cited research. Man cannot be effectively divided into separate spheres, even in the name of religious faith. It is difficult to find a dividing line in the human personality according to which we can set the sacred on one side and the secular on the other. It seems no longer profitable to maintain the old distinctions of mind and body and flesh and spirit which crystallized the antagonisms that estranged man for so long from a proper sense of his own unity. The emerging religious consciousness of our time turns man back to himself, to the task of feeling again the oneness of the personality given to him by God. One can no longer suppose that the religious man searches for a spiritual order that is separate from his own human experience. The unity of life in a totally redeemed universe must be reasserted in order to heal the wound from which man has suffered because of the exaggerated dualism that has disembodied the things of the spirit for such a long time. Man cannot be approached only on the spiritual plane. He must be approached as man. Religious categories must be capable of being discussed in terms of human experience in order to end the estrangement that history has introduced into man's sense of his own personality.

Fourthly, serious questions with implications for everything from catechetics to the liturgy must be asked in view of the relationship between full personal growth and a well-developed religious faith. The reason is clear: Most people do not possess a fully developed personality and do not have a fully developed religious faith either. Those who are alive psychologically and religiously may be close relatives to the individuals who are categorized as *developing* in the study of American priests. They are, in a respected ascetical phrase, "in via." They understand that the Christian journey is one of growth toward a goal they have not yet achieved. The excitement lies in the possibility and promise of the goal, in the conviction that it endures against the ravages of time and space, and in the commitment to the experiences that bring human beings closer to it. Is it impossible, one might ask, for a severely neurotic person to have mature faith? It may well be, but it is not impossible for a neurotic to have a maturing faith. If the Christian life is a dynamic, process-oriented experience built on the unitary nature of personality, then these ideas need not estrange us from traditional positions. Indeed, one might return to the history of ascetic literature in order to rediscover the images of growth that have always pervaded it. The understanding that man is made to grow and to fulfill a destiny that is at once religious and personal is hardly a new idea to anyone who has ever read the New Testament.

Chapter Five

DOUBTING

Faith and doubt have traditionally been contrasted with one another. We are familiar with the hesitations that earned the apostle the title, "Doubting Thomas." Then there is the indictment of certain people because they seem to have "little faith." On the other hand, the proverb tells us belief is strong enough to move mountains. What, in an age of sophisticated inquiry and discovery, can all this mean for modern man? Can he, in fact, believe at all if he is subject to doubts; or can he achieve any depth of belief if he does not doubt?

Doubt has generally been presented as a failure, not just of nerve but of the whole believing system, something like a moral fault for which a person must be held accountable. There is, for example, an idea of doubt as a conscious choice not to believe, a deliberate flirtation with the rejection of religious faith. This type of doubt is always considered to be destructive, something dangerous in the air like an infection that eats away at the foundations of religious institutions. There is a public character to this kind of doubt, a kind of notoriety through which an individual defines himself against the Church of which he has been a member. The person who doubts this way invites censure from his religious group and may even be labeled a heretic or an apostate, the indications that doubt has exploded within the individual into positive unbelief.

Doubt has also been associated with a kind of weakness that carries the implication of a dissolving moral fiber or at least some self-indulgence in wavering thoughts about faith. This doubt is judged a personal rather than a public failure.

Those guilty of it seldom earn the censure of their religious institutions. These people do not seem vitally concerned with official Church affiliation; they seem to be individuals in whose lives formal religion does not make any decisive difference. In the judgment of self-styled true believers, they seem to have made friends with the world rather than with God. There are many variations on this theme, of course, and these people are generally prayed for rather than condemned.

Doubt has also been popularly considered as a species of temptation, a presentation in an attractive way of the alternative of non-belief, the choice of which would constitute a major sin. Here again we have a private rather than a public choice through which an individual aligns himself with the forces opposed to those of righteousness and fidelity. This temptation may float into a person's consciousness because of pernicious teachers, godless scientists, atheistic revolutionaries, or some other easily categorized group who seem at odds with the traditional expressions of faith. Doubt as temptation comes to the young man who goes off to college, or falls in with unbelieving companions, and finally gives up his faith much to the consternation of his clergyman and his family. Such a loss must be admitted and confessed if the person is to reintegrate himself with the group of believers from which he has separated himself. Only the institution can absolve and readmit him for this breach of believing.

Doubt, in any of these guises, has always had a bad name. However, modern men cannot look at doubt in an oversimplified and negative fashion. It may be true that ten thousand questions, as Cardinal Newman said, do not constitute a single doubt, but would any good questions ever be asked if a person did not doubt something about his environment at one time or another? The Christian life is poorly served by those models that portray it as a determined march forward of Christians with jaws set, eyes unblinking, and mind closed against all questions or uneasiness. Such unwavering belief bellows to us to walk through the valley of death without fear because of our trust in God. Such serenity, however, may come only to the individual who has, in fact, had to ask very serious and probing questions about the beliefs that explain the universe and the incidents of his own life to him. It may be inhuman and insensitive not to raise questions or to still the spirit of wonder about life and our religious interpretations of it.

A Church denies the right of its poets to question at great danger to itself. Poetry is, after all, the native language of faith. So the poets who ride before us into the darkness sense and deal with significant human question far in advance of most of us. They do this not out of intellectual pride but out of constitutional necessity, because they are attuned to the developing situations that ultimately will touch and affect all men. Can the language of myth, which has preserved the meanings of faith so powerfully across the centuries, be spoken by the individual who has committed himself to an excessive literalism about life? Can the poet or the prophet promise not to doubt? It is difficult to accept the dull rhythms that reassure us when there are times in history when we cannot get by without the unsettling questions of the poets. The poets, whether they are theologians or prelates (and the odds are against this happy combination), cannot perform their function of alerting us to the meanings of our world unless they are permitted to ask what would seem to be doubting questions.

There is surely some comfort in not doubting, a security akin to that which we think we provide when we buy double locks against the burglars who are more clever than we are. Our security is spurious, and, in the long run, something that plays into the hands of those who would despoil us. Not asking questions has never been a good defense against the mystery of life. Another difficulty connected with this is the tone of judgmental righteousness which is found in the condemning pronouncements of self-styled true believers. True believers, or those in charge of orthodoxy throughout history, have always seemed very hard on man. To raise difficult issues seems to fit the curious nature of man. A system of belief that has no room for questions leaves very little room for man himself.

It has been difficult for many persons even to think about doubt or to examine some of their inner questionings very closely. There are many reasons for this, including the fact that belief in a strong institutional Church may have exercised extensive if very subtle control over their behavior in the formative stages of their lives. The Catholic Church is a good example of this because, in a fashion that would surely anticipate the work of psychologist B. F. Skinner, many Catholics became self-monitoring. The system of control was so extensive, in other words, that they did not even need supervision in order to maintain themselves within the boundary of acceptable reflection about their faith. The guilt attached to doubting—or to other forms of presumably unacceptable thought or fantasy—was sufficient punishment in itself to bring the person back into the acceptable boundaries of his own self-examination. The reward of avoiding this guilt was actually the major positive reinforcer of orthodoxy. This kind of control is extraordinarily advantageous to the institution and, if we focus only on behavior, benefits the individual because it deepens his sense of participation in a meaningful system and prevents him from getting too involved in painful conflicts.

Indeed, conflict became the experience for those who persisted in questioning systems of discipline or the phrasing of articles of belief that were totally accepted by most churchgoers. Doubters would exile themselves or find themselves exiled. Because of their inherent need to question it is not surprising to find that many artists, writers, and poets moved outside the institutional Church despite their clear connections and fascination with the Catholic tradition.

There is a psychological factor operative in most persons that keeps them from disturbing the waters of their belief systems too much. To question the interpretations of the

world which we receive in our childhood leads to a disloca-
tion of our entire universe. While many people may be
curious, they are not anxious to cause themselves unneeded
pain by sifting through their beliefs with too much alertness.
They do not want to activate any stern test of their belief
if they can avoid it. They may not believe everything as it
was once told to them, but they are not willing—or perhaps
are unable psychologically—to state loudly and clearly that
they now question seriously or even reject these beliefs.
There seems to be no need for it if the beliefs, in general,
seem to serve their religious needs fairly well. This is not to
say that all tests can be avoided; life provides them in
illness, tragedies, and a variety of challenging circumstances
all the time. These individuals, however, do not wish to be
placed in the witness box about their commitment to literal
interpretations of belief. They can pass as believers, and, in
fact, their true faith may be rather lively. It is simply that
the narrow definitions which have put such a premium on
literal concepts of faith seem fragile symbols to them and
they do not want to poke into them or dislodge them un-
necessarily. They do not care to become public or even
private doubters because the potential pain outweighs the
possible discoveries that they might thereby make. They
would prefer, quite in private, to have a sliding scale of investment in the literal claims of institutional religions. They
doubt, but very quietly.

Doubt remains in the guise of an enemy, or at least an
unwelcome stranger from whom you keep at a safe distance.
If doubt is an enemy, then it is appropriate to ignore or to
crush it immediately. Such have been the strategies employed in the broad treatment of religious doubt through
the centuries. Nevertheless, not all doubt is an enemy or
even a stranger to human nature or to faith. As in many
other spheres of human activity, doubt may be a positive
function of a personality that is engaged in a meaningful
way with life. Doubt can be an aspect of healthy curiosity
as well as a sign of our seemingly inborn tendency to explore; these responses are very natural and extremely im-

portant for man. It is itself doubtful that man could survive very long if he were not capable of questioning his view of things or if he were not open to new signals and new interpretations of reality around him. He would certainly not discover anything, or express any creativity; on the level of physical survival alone he might not last very long. Doubt, pesky and irritating though it sometimes seems, may be an important referent for the developing personality. When an individual seeks for a true sense of himself doubt may be best considered, as stated by Philip M. Helfaer, as an aspect of the ego seeking a full synthesis of itself.[1]

Indeed, modern man, instead of having his tendency to question suppressed, may need encouragement to ask the right questions and to search courageously for more satisfactory answers. The possibility of doubt as an aspect of healthy self-integration must be viewed again when so many literal beliefs are no longer accepted by a better-educated and more-sophisticated world. As man stands on the threshold of his new home in the stars he is, consciously or not, putting aside the representations of the universe which divided it into the antagonistic elements of heaven and earth. Indeed, he finds less believable all those interpretations that make so many subdivisions in man's perception of himself and the world around him. When certain statements of faith no longer explain the experience of life satisfactorily, man cannot keep himself from doubting. It is an integral part of his search for a more adequate understanding of the meaning of his life. This is part of the genius of his religious imagination and his capacity for discovery, a powerful ally in his efforts to theologize sensitively about life.

Doubt cannot help but come into an individual's life when institutional Churches continue to offer interpretations of life that no longer match his own experience or knowledge. This, of course, is the cutting edge of belief itself, a profound aspect of human growth. The individual who is in touch with his experience does not readily accept an interpretation that contradicts it, attempts to suppress it, or

[1] *The Psychology of Religious Doubt* (Boston: Beacon Press, 1972).

seems to make little of its character. Reactive doubt is inevitable in such situations: "How can I believe what I know cannot be true?" a person asks in this situation. This doubt is not unhealthy because it means an individual is accepting responsibility for what he believes in. He does not easily surrender his own convictions when these are not capricious, the fruit of unacknowledged rebellion, or evidence of some other psychological difficulty of his own. It is this sense of experience's claims on us—rather than science—which topples the authoritarian insistence on a single view of life. This is not to say, of course, that man's questioning curiosity inevitably destroys any and every religious belief he may have known in his life. It does, however, challenge the Churches to look more deeply into the statement of their beliefs and to examine their imagery and symbolism, so that they can continue to speak the primary truths of faith to man in relevant and understandable language. It is right here, however, where the issue must be met head on, where we have to question our inherited belief systems in terms of our own experience. After everything is sorted out, after all the reassuring answers have been given, the question becomes for each of us, "What do I really believe in?"

This question disturbs us because it may lead us to a reordering of our interpretation of the world and, therefore, to a restructuring of our own lives. The question does not ask what we accept on the word of authority, or what we believe, because to disbelieve would cause pain to those we love; the question directs us to the convictions on the basis of which we lead our lives. It refers us to operational faith, to the principles that guide us in our attitude toward ourselves, our work, and those close to us. It bids us to inspect our attitudes to see whether they are undergirded by any consistent and embracing philosophy or theology of the world. The honest man begins by discovering the things in which he truly believes; these may be quite different from the things in which he professes belief on a more surface level.

In response to this kind of inquiry some would provide

the answer that what man must believe in is the creed of the Church. In fact, this is the very strategy that has been used in recent years by certain members of the hierarchy of the Roman Catholic Church. This emphasis on objective belief tends to separate it from the life experience of the believer; this re-creates, in other words, the old mistake of thinking that so-called "religious" element of personality can be abstracted from our motivational system, and that thus excised, it will respond better to creeds enforced with purposeful discipline. This is an institutional response to anxiety, to the kind of worry that creeps into the souls of men when their belief systems are questioned. A difficult state of affairs, no doubt, but it is surely not an abnormal one, nor should it immediately be condemned under the old rubric that doubt and questioning are intrinsically evil. It is not really to deepen faith but to allay anxiety that ecclesiastics have spoken of an "irreducible minimum" in which a person must believe in order to count himself as a member of the Roman Catholic Church. This is to underscore the objective nature of belief in a manner that destroys the rhythmic interaction between believer and belief that is essential to a personal religious response.

The advantages of an irreducible minimum are, however, very great. This reassures the institution that it knows what it is about, that it is in continuity with its tradition, and that it has not been guilty of misinforming or misleading its believers. It also reassures the institution in terms of its authority and continues a flexing of its orthodox muscles as it reaches out to keep its own believers in a properly responsive stance to its pronouncements. This is enormously helpful to some individuals who are in crisis about what they believe in. If the Church is there, rising above the post-industrial world as a serene and reassuring presence, then their doubts, or even their need to inspect them, may safely be put aside. These believers find comfort in believing that things do not change in a changing world.

In many ways this emphasis on certain articles of faith leads to an exaggerated and distorted ordering of beliefs, an outcome of an unconscious need for discipline and institutional order rather than orthodox purity. Such, for example, is the Roman Catholic Church's continued insistence on the discipline of celibacy for its priests. This is on the practical level one of the few things in which a person must believe at the present time. Although this is an extremely strange state of affairs, it is one which ecclesiastics do not wish to examine too deeply. Neither do they wish to examine too carefully the theology of the Church, the priesthood, or the episcopacy because, at some level of their awareness, they know that such a re-examination may challenge the beliefs they now hold on these matters. While there is wide-ranging theological speculation on many matters within the Catholic Church at the present time, celibacy is in right focus because it is one of the few areas in which the authorities of the Church can effectively assert themselves. This reveals how churchmen can make themselves unbelievable when they do not keep up with their theological, scriptural, or historical studies. They can only defend a tradition built on previous and less-sensitive theological and scriptural foundations. When celibacy becomes everything the meaning of faith as a total personal response to life is markedly diminished.

Another difficulty connected with the insistence on an irreducible minimum is that it places enormous burden on the individual. Must he, in the face of his conscience and careful reflection, force his experiences into a scheme of religious interpretation which simply does not explain them anymore? Is that really the burden of the individual, to go on accepting, even at the price of personal conflict, statements in which he can no longer believe? The burden, I suggest, is rather on the Churches who commit their theologians, not merely to restate old beliefs, but to help all men recognize constantly renewing face of perennial belief. The individual is indeed in a difficult situation when he hears, from very high sources in the Church, statements which reflect a somewhat primitive, externalized, and immature concept of the world of human experience. It does not help, for example, to have the Pope speaking about the reality of an individual devil in an age in which it is urgently important for people to come to terms with the evil of which they themselves are capable. To underscore a devil outside of us is to locate evil outside of ourselves and to excuse us from the penetrating self-confrontation that is essential to a growing faith. A reassertion of a literal devil is a throwback that makes it harder than easier to understand the problem of evil.

Helfaer distinguishes two approaches to religious doubt, building on the contrast found between the outlooks of Karl Barth and Paul Tillich. For Barth, a more fundamentalistic theologian, doubt was a betrayal. Of it, he says that "no one should flirt with his unbelief or with his doubt—theologians should only be sincerely ashamed of it."[2] On the other hand, Tillich says that "if doubt appears, it should not be considered as the negation of faith, but as an intrinsic element which was always and will always be present in the active faith."[3] Helfaer, in his brilliant analysis of religious doubt, contrasts two psychological types who are characteristic, in the practical order, of the differing viewpoints of these two great Protestant theologians. The conservative position in theology, he suggests, is ordered to the reduction of the ambiguity found in the symbols of the religious belief system. The doctrines of the belief system are then applied as absolutes to the personality. The liberal position, however, permits far more individual interpretation of the symbols of faith, especially as they relate to a person's own experience. "In conservative theologizing," Helfaer notes, "the doctrines are applied to the person, and if he has experiences which do not fit the doctrines, he is wrong. In the liberal position,

[2] Karl Barth, *Evangelical Theology* (New York: Holt, Rinehart and Winston, 1963), p. 131.

[3] Paul Tillich, *The Dynamics of Faith* (New York: Harper & Bros., 1957), p. 22.

the individual's experience is more a key to interpreting the religious symbols."[4]

He believes that these approaches, which find their origins in the psychological history of the individuals in whom they are expressed, correspond roughly to the processes of internalization and externalization that have already been applied to the analysis of religious faith. These flow, not in some judgmental sense about the value of one position over the other, but as a consequence of the life history of the individual and in his particular efforts to understand who he is and to define himself in place and time in a meaningful way. Helfaer is careful not to pass judgment, as though he were denigrating the conservative position to exalt the liberal view of developmental faith. In fact, he takes pains to avoid this. It is obvious, however, that he finds an acceptable and positive place for doubt in the development of a faith system and that he sees the task of the maturing individual as tied up with a steady self-examination of his own belief.

It is difficult to see how man can achieve a higher synthesis of himself if he is not permitted to question or reassess his motives or his understanding of life. The mature believer needs to doubt in order to get in better touch with himself and to make his believing more responsive to the reality of his own life and to that of the world around him. This kind of doubt, found in striving persons everywhere, seems to be an aspect of our search for wholeness. Doubt is, however, not merely a careless attitude toward religion or its symbols. It is a painful and difficult process, involving self-confrontation and requiring a serious commitment of the person to the process. It also needs an environment in which it can be carried out without excessive threat being present. In other words, the believer must be helped to believe enough in his own searchings so that he can follow them through with honesty and thoroughness. These are weighty conditions to achieve.

[4] Helfaer, op. cit., p. 54.

Growing believers need a Church which is sensitive enough to their needs and rich enough in its symbols to allow this search to proceed, even on an individual basis, without too much repression out of fear that its own institutional integrity may be damaged. The Churches, in other words, need a more profound faith in man. The question is not whether men believe in the Churches but whether the Churches believe in them. Nor is the question whether the Church has a future but whether the Church believes that man has a future. Any Church that represses its capacity to question also cripples its capacity to learn; it may, in the process, severely damage its claims to teach. The issue is one of believability. A Church reveals itself as something we can believe in when it permits man to be himself and to search, following the rigorous conditions needed to do this with integrity, for the beliefs that will make sense of his own life.

This may require the Churches to confront themselves to see whether their priorities make room for man who must doubt if he is going to grow. If, on the other hand, the Church is more concerned about its own survival than about the growth of man, it can only restrict the possibilities of man's investigation of himself. Actually, it can only try to retard a journey that persons must set out upon if they are to be believers with any depth at all. "Blessed are they who have not seen but have believed," is the phrase that has been used against unbelievers for years. It may well be turned against the Churches who, in their anxiety to repress doubt, have failed to believe in anything but the most literal interpretation of religious faith. This is a foreshortened vision that speaks of an institution that does not believe enough in the things that it cannot see, that may have the eyes of faith but keeps them tightly closed. Man's profound need to believe includes needs to doubt and to inquire. Only a Church that sincerely believes in man as he is and that understands and accepts the rich texture of faith can help human beings to become true believers. The faith that makes men whole makes room for questions and for the blessings of endless discovery and surprise.

Chapter Six

THE FACES OF FIDELITY

To the fabled visitor from another planet, fidelity might seem to be something that everybody talks about but nobody does much about anymore. Although fidelity is still an ideal it is not an absolute requirement in a super-sophisticated world. Fidelity bears the weight of cobwebbed connotations, and strikes many as a quaint notion out of the past when people settled for stable, if sometimes romantically undernourished relationships. Now, however, men and women question lifelong fidelity as though it were a dream of a madman who only confused human affairs by introducing the idea in the first place. Fidelity, which involves a great deal of believing, has been pronounced, or at the very least, is now defined, in terms of a limited span of time.

The question of fidelity is relevant not only to human relationships but also to religious symbolism and the institutional Churches. If men and women are suddenly proclaiming a new freedom from the iron grasp of an old concept of fidelity, they are also questioning ancient formulas of faith and actively turning aside from a whole inventory of respected and presumably stable religious traditions. It is not just the faithfulness of lovers for each other that is under question at this time; it is also man's capacity to believe in God or in his spokesman for any sustained amount of time. Our present conflicts about fidelity affect man's willingness to enter into institutions that expect him to remain in relationship with them for life. A pervasive contemporary problem, fidelity is one of the dimensions of believing which is most important to understand.

The present questioning, of course, does not reflect so

much a desire for limited periods of fidelity in marriage as much as it reveals deep yearning for an unquestioned and permanent fidelity that would be immune to the fierce weathering it experiences in the human condition. Invulnerable fidelity is one person's want, and not getting it, he gives up on fidelity altogether. The virtues of infidelity are discussed because this seems to free persons from the situations and relationships that have not worked out or have gone stale, and in which fidelity is a sterile demand for conformity rather than an incorporation through reciprocal believing into life. The desire for such freedom is a search for something other than the human condition, for a time and place where love won't hurt anymore and where we won't have to recommit ourselves every day to the contingencies of life. In a sense, this longing for a more effortless form of believing—fidelity that takes care of itself—is understandable. The strategy of achieving it by undercutting the very notion of fidelity, however, seems strange indeed.

It is also true that although we might like the freedom to be less obsessively faithful ourselves, we are not quite so ready to permit others to be unfaithful to us. Whether this is compounded of self-pity or accurate self-perception is hard to tell; the fact remains, however, that we are far more tolerant of our own ambivalence toward fidelity than we are of the infidelities of others toward us. There is a large measure of subjective dishonesty symbolized in questioning even the possibility of lifelong fidelity to any promises, whether to marriage, to a belief, or to a vocation in life. Some modern persons are obviously uneasy about their own identities; the cracks in the foundation of fidelity come from the pressures exerted by their own inner problems. Perhaps we should not be surprised that a generation of Americans plagued with self-doubt and identity crises have special problems with the notion of fidelity. Fidelity, the capacity to dedicate oneself to another person or to a cause, has been described as one of the works of adolescence, something one must achieve as a prerequisite for reasonably healthy and

productive participation in the adult world. Our estrangement from fidelity may be a sign that we have not completed
our adolescent growth. The statistics on affairs or about
the older marriages that have become dehydrated and are
blowing away across the continent may tell us that we have
fallen short rather than fidelity itself, and that, in a strange
way, our present discussions point out our need for fidelity
rather than that we have outgrown it.

There is also widespread concern that if the present pub-
licized disenchantment with lifelong fidelity continues,
society itself will come down in a thunderous and final collapse. In these discussions, the young are the ones usually ac-
cused of shaking the beliefs of yesterday by rejecting the
institutions of today. Young couples, for example, question
the idea of entering into marriage until they are sure they
wish to remain with each other; so too, they doubt the value
of attending Church to pay tribute to a belief about which
they have little conviction. These reactions seem alarming
to an older generation that never felt it could afford even
the luxury of asking such questions. Older people, including
many churchmen and good parents, sometimes seem willing to settle for the appearance of fidelity both in marriage
and in church attendance in order to spread some cohesive
paste across the shattered institutions of society. They seem
to believe that a little hypocrisy in the service of stability
may not be such a bad thing after all.

Young people may, however, be stalking the concept of
fidelity, looking for the secret that makes things last, as
earnestly as anyone else in society. Although they seem at
odds with the generation that raised them, their yearning
for stable and emotionally satisfying relationships are not
unlike those of their parents. Some of the conflict comes from
the fact that this issue is so sensitive, springing as it does
from tender depths in the heart, that people defend themselves even as they try to speak about it. The generations
share a sensitivity to and a fear of the potential for hurt
which is involved in the real life working out of fidelity. The

young express a somewhat intuitive hesitation about committing themselves for good before they are emotionally prepared to do so. They also seem to mean it when they speak of wanting relationships marked by the strength of reciprocal caring. Members of the older generation, on the other hand, are reaping the fruits of having entered many marriage relationships before they were ready for them and before they even understood the kind of strength they would need in order to work them through successfully. Some of these older people are only now seeking the kind of relationship marked by a deep and mutual caring, the kind that makes intimacy safe, the very thing they may have missed earlier.

We may have reached the age in which we can finally get beneath the surface of fidelity, in which we can learn something richer and deeper and in better perspective about it than we have been able to do before. We may not have reached the final season of faithfulness, its farewell performance in the human condition, as much as a chance to look at it closely again. What may have been taken for granted too quickly about a fidelity that could never be questioned is now being examined by those who want to get at its core value, if they can find it. Men and women want to unearth the roots of fidelity rather than merely be dazzled by its seasonal blooms. This is not the popular way of looking at our present conflicts over fidelity; the previously cited "Roman Empire Syndrome" is far more the diagnosis of choice. Both marriage and the Churches are falling apart, according to the Sunday supplements; is this true when we look at it more closely? Or are these institutions under stress precisely because men and women seek for an experience of faithfulness that celebrates rather than paralyzes their relationship with each other? It seems hardly unlikely that human beings are giving up on fidelity any more than they are giving up on believing in general. They are rather hoping that they can find a new—and in some cases an easier—brand of fidelity that will serve them, like the psalmist's shield, against all that life can do to vulnerable persons.

In order to understand fidelity or to come closer to a realization of what it demands of us, we must have some understanding of the nature of choice and of the free commitment of ourselves which we make to other persons or
to causes. What is needed is an awareness of the motiva-
tions that drive us in certain directions even when we are
not completely conscious of them. Unless we have some
appreciation of these, of course, we can never expand our
freedom of choice or really commit ourselves to anything.
To become individuals requires a steady increase in our own
sensitivity to ourselves so that we can consciously bring into
better balance our expectations of fidelity from others and
our willingness to respond faithfully to them.

Nor can we be strangers to our own possibilities for deceit, both of ourselves and of others, in the pursuit of temporary and not very satisfying intermediate goals in life. One
of the great psychological mysteries of all times centers on
the way we can, in fact, choose small rewards even though
we know we are going to pay very heavily for these later on.
Man has an elaborate catalogue of defenses, not the least of
which is the polished rationalization that makes everything,
howsoever inconsistent, seem reasonable if not thoughtful.
It is hard to break far enough out of ourselves to get this
tendency into perspective; it is still easy to fool ourselves.
We must not be naïve about the way we can twist the pattern of our own existence or deliberately misread it in an
effort to make the face of reality more comforting to us. We
really never get too old to deceive ourselves and the individual who would master the meaning of fidelity should
never lose sight of this.

An appreciation of fidelity also requires an appreciation
of the nature of commitment; a commitment can never be
effectively defined as something that is done once and forever in life, a point of choice in time when we made some
pledge or promise. Commitments are better understood as
continuing acts of believing. The commitment of ourselves
to others or to institutions requires a full-dimensioned belief

through which we work out our relationships to each other or to these causes afresh every day. As far as commitments go, life begins at dawn for each one of us. We may surround an initial commitment with a ritual and memorialize it in a similar fashion on succeeding anniversaries. These activities, however, are undertaken only to sharpen our focus on the everyday essence of commitment. It is a continuous phenomenon, the meaning of which emerges in the lives of those who know that we do not live on promises made a long time ago but on vows that are deepened with each new day.

The nature of the commitment that enlivens fidelity is not that of some abstract law or prescription handed down by God in the early hours of the human race's existence. Commitment suffers from the clustering burden of historical settings and examples. Essentially, commitment is centered in a living and developing personal belief in another person. Commitment is not found in any other form, even though it may be formalized by an institution such as a Church, or spoken of in relationship to the traditions of a race or a family. Commitment is intrinsically personal, always bringing us face to face with another individual and summoning from us the level of response needed in this situation. Committing ourselves to each other is always filled with hazards and difficulties because we change so through time; we grow wiser, get sick, change jobs, and move to different localities; we get a new look at things, including ourselves, and we cannot avoid becoming different and, to a certain extent, even estranged from the self we knew at an earlier time. On this strange moving edge of life we meet and commit ourselves to each other. Such commitment has meaning when we appreciate and make room for the changes that will necessarily occur in ourselves and in those around us. Sometimes surprising and sometimes expected, they are predictably constant. Fundamentally, our commitment is to growth, to becoming more of ourselves and with an increasing sensitivity to each other. Commitments live in a human setting; that is why they tap into our personal capacity to believe. We live out our commitments through operational belief in each other.

The believing that goes with living fidelity builds on our changeableness in a positive and constructive way. Fidelity that depends on deadened adjustment resembles an uneasy peace in Northern Ireland or in the Middle East. Anything can disrupt it at any moment. That is why people sometimes feel trapped by fidelity; it seems like a suffocating cloak rather than an aspect of their experience through which they freely express and expand themselves. To respond with faithfulness means to continue to change in accord with the changes in oneself and in one's loved ones. None of this is accomplished without sensitivity, communication, and the willingness to make sacrifices in order to share what truly happens in and through one's life experience. This is the kind of fidelity in which people grow together; it does not freeze them in space and time but makes room for them to become more mature, to experience unpredictable difficulties and unexpected problems, to grow occasionally at differing rates so that their need to respond to each other becomes more urgent and, in the long run, more fruitful. This fidelity depends on an understanding of one of believing's essential characteristics, its capacity to grow to match the needs and transformations of personality.

Belief is centered not on what we were when we first met, nor what we were on our wedding day, our time of ordination or religious profession, or some other occasion on which we crystallized in a single moment our commitment. Fundamentally, our belief is in what we can become together, through our reciprocal commitment to growth under the influence of the Spirit. Our commitment, in the long run, is to this reality, one that never takes care of itself. Belief, contrary to some understandings of it, is not something which, once secured, takes care of us. It is something we work on all the time, a mystery that demands a constant incorporation of the truth of ourselves into the heart of our relationships of fidelity. Fidelity is not, then, just a stern command never to change but rather a very complicated invitation to continue to grow at the price of changing to some extent each day. This is the way fidelity is kept fresh, the way human beings are unable to stay alive and to grow together through a life time.

It may be easy enough to apply this to the relationship of friendship or to a marriage, but it is also important to consider this in relationship to institutions like the Church. The administrators of these institutions refer to their communicants as "the faithful." They tend to demand certain regular responses that demonstrate the fidelity these people have toward the Church's teachings and its moral and dogmatic guidelines and instructions. The dynamics of fidelity obtain in the relationship between an individual and his Church in much the way they do between an individual and the one he loves. Fidelity is reciprocal wherever it is found, and as the burden can be placed fairly on neither the husband nor the wife alone, so the burden for fidelity cannot safely be placed fully on the faithful. The other side of the issue asks the Churches to be faithful, not just to their historical past nor to their traditions, but to the living experience of growing more deeply in their commitment of service and love to their people. The Church's commitment is worked out every day, more personally than officially, when it is pastorally alive to today's men and women.

The essential Church is, of course, alive whenever human beings themselves are alive to each other. The administrative Church, however, needs to look more deeply at its own commitment of fidelity and at the way it responds to its people. The Church can fail in faith, in other words, through an inherent slowness or a reluctance to keep faith with the overall growth of its people. The feeling of estrangement that fills the corridors of many institutional Churches springs from the difficulties these Churches habitually get into by trying to define too rigidly the nature of their relationship to their people. These Churches become estranged because they either never knew or else they have forgotten that their commitment is not to the changeless requirements of membership lists but to growing persons in whom the essence of belief truly lives.

What kills the kind of fidelity that should be found in Churches is the previously mentioned confusion of the notions of loyalty and fidelity. Blind obedience is just not the same as active and searching believing. Fidelity makes room for the latter but not for the former. Loyalty of this kind kills faith and fidelity. Fidelity belongs to the living, to those who still love enough to respond to the impulses of growth even when these demand a constant self-transformation. A Church is faithful not by refusing to change but by being willing to grow.

The problems of fidelity for institutions are as difficult as they are for individuals. Essentially, however, they are the same. That means that they are intrinsically personal, that they are rooted in the process of continuing growth and developing consciousness that marks the passage of men through life and history. The Churches cannot be faithful unless they are ready always to speak in new languages in order to respond with a full and living faith to the believers they serve. To fail to hear contemporary man's cries for a richer and deeper grasp of what it means to be faithful and to believe is to misunderstand, misdefine, and ultimately to miss altogether the challenge of fidelity in modern life.

II

BELIEVERS

BELIEVERS

As I noted in the Introduction to this book, the following interviews do not comprise a representational sample of human beliefs. They are a sampling rather than a sample and no generalizations can be made from them. I asked a number of well-known people if they would be willing to speak about the subject of believing, and these chapters record my meetings with them and their own reflections on the subject. The fact that some of these people are well known does not make them better believers, although I think it adds a dimension of interest and adds to our evidence about the pervasive quality of belief. They all believe in something and I think each of us has much to learn from listening to what others say about the faith by which they lead their lives. This can light up our own faith and traditions and encourage us to search ourselves for those beliefs to which we are really committed.

I have tried to present these people in the context of their lives, to open a view of these persons that makes them more alive and permits us to see some section of the worlds in which they live and work. This is necessarily to present them as they struck me, to share, in other words, what I saw and sensed in my own fallible journalistic way. In the main, however, it is an effort to allow them to speak for themselves and to take us with them as they examine something of what they believe in.

Notre Dame's golden dome rides atop a big old-fashioned building filled with Holland Tunnel sized hallways and fifteen foot high doors that must have been painted a dozen times since Harding died. The office of Father Theodore Hesburgh, president of the University, is done in a battleship gray that seems favored in older Catholic institutions. The waiting room is simple with nondescript carpeting and old furniture that does not quite match. It is clear that Father Hesburgh does not depend upon artifice to define himself or the power he wields as an educator who is perhaps the best-known and most influential priest in the United States.

His office is cluttered and manly, the setting for work into the small hours of the morning as well as the meetings and other activities that consume a university president's day. Father Hesburgh greets me and, explaining that he has had no time for lunch, goes into a side room to prepare himself a cup of soup. He returns and, switching his stereo set on with a remote control device, sits behind his desk and begins to reflect on the subject of believing. He is assured and friendly, a man who has been everywhere and seen everything. "What is faith all about? I see it as an opening, a window, a door on an entirely different world than the world of secular reality. It doesn't downplay this world or make it less important." He sips his steaming minestrone carefully. "But it provides us with a surrounding framework of beliefs that make all other things make sense. Faith gives us another sense of relationship to the secular world. It integrates it on a deep level and provides a source of meaning. Faith opens us to that whole world that gives ultimate meaning to what we do."

Father Hesburgh leans back and clasps his hands behind his head revealing a copper wrist bracelet like those worn by golfers and other athletes. Gazing across the room which looks like a harbor filled with mementos riding at anchor, he continues. "I can't think about faith all the time, but I would say it is the kind of thing that I am at home with. If you strip faith out of my life, then you are taking something very vital out of it. Faith is a part of a man's total make-up. It is the dimension that pulls things together. That faith is revealed in what you do. Take the Mass, for example. For me, offering Mass has to be as normal as eating or breathing, something that you do every day. It is an expression of the faith by which you lead your life. You know," and he unclasps his hands from behind his head and leans forward, "I have only missed Mass one day in thirty years as a priest, and I've been in a lot of odd-ball places and had to stretch the rules about it in the early days. But the Mass is central just as salvation is central for the human race. When I offer Mass I put myself in relationship to the human race. I can reach back to all the dead, and I can respond to the yearning of the world, to all those whose faith is known to God alone. I can also touch the future. I think that prayer in the Mass sums it up: 'Let us proclaim the mystery of faith: Christ has died, Christ has risen, Christ will come again.'

"There is a lot of looking forward involved in this for the Christian. Many people think of eschatology, the last things, as some mass mob scene in a football stadium with Christ standing on the fifty-yard line waiting to judge us all. But in the hour of death we will meet him and this will reveal what we now take on faith. I think this perspective on history is very much needed in the world of faith. That is what the Mass allows us to do, embrace all of time. This is very much what I think Teilhard de Chardin was getting at. There is a lot of him that I don't like, but he gives you a sense of participation in the developing history of the world.

The Mass enables us to touch it all every day in the act of salvation. My days are usually filled to the hilt with secular reality, but at the moment of Mass I can touch the core of what the world is all about. For me a day without that would be a day not being a priest. It is a foundation stone. I do it because I am not holy. I even say Mass alone if it is impossible for me to celebrate it with a community. Thinking of all the needs of the world enables me to pull together the communal nature of the act. It is very important to me so that wherever I am and whatever I am doing, I know that I am going to say Mass. I just don't think you can be a priest unless you remind yourself in a powerful and functional way every day that you are a priest.

"It is connected with the nature of offering sacrifice. We have to give up our will in some way. What the heck are you a priest for? We must be all caught up in the living act of salvation. Now, by saying this I certainly don't want to sit in judgment on anyone. I am just saying what is important in my faith. Without these I would be a poor man as a priest with the life that I lead. But the Mass and the Office are the two links that I have for the power of salvation and the power of personal grace. Otherwise my life would be a totally secular thing. If somebody wanted to fault me they could say that something I did was unpriestly. I would hate to think of doing anything without trying to have it as part of my priestly activity, without it being open to this reality.

"I have actually spent my whole life on the fringes of the Church. Most of the things that I have been a part of, I have not only been the only priest but the only Catholic present. And my value to these people on committees and commissions—aside from my value as a friend—came from trying to bring some deeper dimension of faith. I was always welcome because I was supposed to represent this dimension. Now these people didn't expect me to express belief in the Trinity, I don't mean that. But they did expect that I would reveal the human values that the Gospel illumines for us. When we were having voter's registration hearings in the South, for example, one of the Civil Rights Commission members said to me, 'Padre, give them a little Christianity.' That was right. These people in the South remember their Bible and they would say to me, 'I know you're right but I just can't change my feelings.'

"The thing that I find curious—or maybe it isn't so curious—is that I know a lot of people who are very good and who do not profess any specific faith. They don't seem to have any deep or abiding faith. These are the people whose faith is known to God alone. They are involved in transcendent things, and I am sure that gets back to God."

Father Hesburgh finishes his soup and pauses for a thoughtful moment, "I find it hard to see how people can live just for time, just for this world. If God makes any sense out of this world, he is going to have to do it in eternity. Evil is so prevalent! At its worst, you see it in the insensitivity to humanity that is all around us, in the injustice even on the material level where we deny people food and clothing, the things that are fundamental to human dignity. You see it in the total dependency of the poor and the total dependency of the oppressed. The sins against these people are the ones that cry to heaven for vengeance. Without faith I don't think there is any answer to the problem of evil, and I know a lot of people who have written God off precisely because they cannot equate a loving God with the amount of evil we see in the world."

I ask him, in view of this, what he would like to see the graduating students at Notre Dame believe in. "I would like them to believe in Christ as the Lord and Savior, to have a commitment to the person of Christ so that they will serve him in the poor and suffering of this world. I think the Notre Dame graduate should have a sense of the presence of the hand of God in his life and realize that he is not just a chip on a turbulent river. I would like to have the average Notre Dame student have a deep belief in eternal life, a sense that his life is a journey to somewhere, that it isn't all just accidental. The young have an enormous belief in Christian service and in finding Christ through serving others. I think they really are struggling for a Christian interpretation of life; something that will help them to make a better world. One of the nice things about our students is that when they criticize us they charge that we are not Christian enough around here. That tells something about their yearning for faith and its values. What I tell them is that if I could wish one thing, it would be that Notre Dame could be a community where people would love each other and take care of each other. We've been one hundred and twenty-five years without a suicide; I think you can only explain that because we have a caring community, that we have people here who are present to care. That is the beauty of this place; it is the symphony of people from many different backgrounds who are all able to respond to each other."

Father Hesburgh hunches together in concentration and turns directly toward me, "You know a young student said to me the other night right in this office, 'It's none of your business if I sleep with a girl.' And I said, 'Maybe that's right, but it's part of my concern. In addition to your attitude toward women, it's important for me to care about the values by which you lead your life, and whether you use them or not. It may not be my business, but it is my business to care.' I think it is a terrible thing in universities today where they have dropped the *in loco parentis*. It is part of the overall problem where they just leave these young people on their own without any guideposts, without anybody to test their ideas on.

"People tend to think of faith vertically, but if you really believe in Christ, if you really believe in the Incarnation, you understand that the vertical dimension is only meaningful if it is expressed horizontally. You have to have faith in what man can be if he is cared for. I think there is a terrible lack of faith when a university says, 'We'll take care of your mind,' and cannot see how much they must care for the whole person. That is why I think we must tell our students that it does matter how they live now, that it is something about which we must be concerned. They are laying the roots for the kind of lives they are going to live later on. What is it Maritain says about man, 'A touch of straw, a touch of fire'? We have to have faith in what these men can be. We can't let them be lost on all the important issues in life.

"I think of Halberstam's book, *The Best and the Brightest*. You could have the best and the brightest in the world, and they can come to rational and intellectual convictions that are very clear. Unless, however, they raise themselves to a higher dimension, to a moral one, they can cause pretty bad disasters. Theirs can be a perceptual, technical brightness, but they miss everything if they are not morally alert on the meaning of right and wrong."

I ask Father Hesburgh about his past 1972 election request for resignation from the chairmanship of the Civil Rights Commission, one of the first actions taken after his re-election by President Nixon. He smiles, a little ruefully it seems to me, and goes on, "Well, the question isn't about me but what it means about American society. As far as the Administration goes, I think I am probably better outside than in it. Thoreau once said that the best place for a man when the government is unjust is in jail. Being cut off like this is a way of saying to me, 'You're not so bad.'

"The great problem of our age, as I see it, is anomie, a restlessness, a lack of faith, a sense of drift. It is no accident that the symbol of faith is an anchor. We need a few anchors of faith to the windward. The extent to which a nation moves away from its anchors of faith, to that extent it will substitute bad surrogates, like superstition creating a faith where faith has been lost. Instead of faith based on the Incarnation, you have a pseudo faith based on magic and other things like that. Man always needs to believe in something."

Father Hesburgh obviously feels deeply about these questions as he rests his arm on his desk and speaks as though to an audience beyond me, "We need a lot of leadership at this time. One of our big problems is that there's not much faith in our leaders, and it's because our leaders don't have vision. They try to operate by a very superficial kind of faith. People in general are really better than they get credit for. They will rarely let you down if you appeal to what is great and noble in them. If you appeal to selfishness or prejudice, then they are going to become this way. They need inspiration rather than to have somebody play to the lowest common denominator about them. I think the greatest fault in our leaders is that they really don't believe in man. We are living in the age of midgets. The fact is that there were great periods of Adenauer, de Gasparri, Roosevelt, Churchill, even Stalin. Think of the great men at the beginning of our country. There is no question that Roosevelt lifted us up as a people in a difficult time or that Churchill did the same thing for the British. Look at what Adenauer did for the battered down people of Germany. But when I hear the name Pompidou I think of some kind of perfume and the name Heath suggests kidney pie. They're just not in the same class. All great leaders had faith in their people and in the rightness of a cause. Something had to be there, something more than just manipulating people. Faith links leadership with vision. That's what Martin Luther King did as he lifted up a whole people, sharing his vision with them. 'I've been to the mountain top and I've seen the promised land . . .'"

I ask him about his own work at the university. "I've got to believe that this is going to be a great Catholic or Christian university or I wouldn't come to work in the morning. Despite the ups and downs, we have the potential of leading men to good here, of doing something about the evil in the world. That is what gives meaning to everything we are trying to do. The trouble with some people is that they get too hung up on specifics. When you ask about faith you don't just ask whether the people believe in the Trinity or original sin. Sometimes that kind of statement doesn't have anything to do with faith. The faith we need now most of all is faith in the Holy Spirit. This is very important in a time of such enormous change, a time in which none of us is wise enough to know what the right decisions are. It must be a terrible time to be a bishop and to think one has to make all these decisions. That's why some of them hole up and avoid it and others try to decide everything in black and white terms. In the very real sense, the best thing we can do today, as we face these problems, is pray, 'Lead Kindly Light.' I think in the Church people ought to use the Gamaliel principle, that a good thing will endure and a bad thing will fall of its own weight. Give it time to work itself out. At this time you just have to believe in the Spirit. The Lord sent his Spirit to strengthen and guide us. There is a need for a special kind of faith in that Spirit. I guess what I try to do in difficult times is say a prayer and follow my instincts.

"We all need a few absolutes, there is no doubt about that. Faith does provide these, but faith in the Spirit adds a suppleness that takes the flinty hardness out of that kind of old-fashioned faith. The Christian's life is marked by a constant effort to be open to the Spirit."

How do you hear the Spirit, I ask Father Hesburgh, who answers immediately, "In humility, in approaching things as though we had something to learn. You know the Church suffers from over-administration. Maybe once in a while, instead of seeming to say the last word on a subject, we could just say that we really don't understand. I have faith that the Church will get leadership, if not from traditional sources, then from others, from lay people who have provided a lot of leadership all through the history of the Church. Part of believing in the Spirit at this time is believing that leadership will come."

I question Father Hesburgh about the future of the Church, and with obvious enthusiasm, he goes on to share his vision of what is happening in Christianity, "We're moving toward one great Christian Church in which we will share belief totally with a great variety of life-styles and liturgies. I think it will be a Church where there will be much more unity than uniformity. I remember being in an ecumenical service recently where a great number of us from different Churches said the Creed together. It struck me then that we really are already able to say the same Creed together. The Spirit is really moving us this way and there are very few obstacles to some official recognition that this Church exists. There are moral issues, of course, but we've been kidding ourselves about being unified on these within the Catholic Church itself. When you think that a third of the world is Christian and that all believe in salvation, redemption, and the grace of God, then you have some sense on how powerfully real this is. The basis of unity is there. I really can't believe that right now we are any less unified than Christianity was in the Diaspora of the first few centuries." Father Hesburgh speaks swiftly as he continues on this theme, "We must give leadership to this movement. There is much more unity on a personal level than you can perceive on an organizational level. I don't think we can wait until the organizations are able to recognize just how close all of us are. We have to leap beyond that past history. Other denominations do not have so much difficulty in accepting the notion of the primacy of the Pope, not now that the theme of collegiality has been stressed. We have to face the fact that there is going to be a sticky period about sex and marriage for the next century. But men and women of all faiths will be praying and working together on the important problems of the world. It is hard to see them working and praying together and not communicating together, not sharing the Eucharist together. That just doesn't make sense.

"Ecumenism is being settled on the grass-roots level, in a very pragmatic way. People on the grass-roots level have a very profound sense of the rightness and wrongness of their worshiping and communicating together. But we so stressed walls without windows that it is hard for us to come to a realization of this. I think the Spirit is blowing down some of these walls. Anybody who argues against Communion in the hand has brought up an idiotic issue. In all these areas the big thing is to know what is important; to receive Christ is what is important. How we do it is not important at all. It's just silly to argue about these things.

"What is genuinely human really cannot be faulted, and that is what we really must follow. I think that's what John did. He made a broad leap on the basis of his sense of history. He did that when he called the Vatican Council to do something about the crime of four hundred and fifty years without any change. We've been trying to cram all that change into ten years, and it has been pretty hard. That's one of the problems now. The faith we gave to people was one that required little from them but to lean on the walls of the institution. Now that those walls have shaken some, they have lost their faith. Well, we never gave them much to begin with.

"In a way, imagining a great catastrophe is a good way to check on your life. Suppose something happened, some great earthquake or something like that. The question is what would be important to do. I think it would be to be together with each other in faith, supplementing each other in love. This is a kind of a science fiction scenario that tells us what we really believe in, the kind of things that really hold us together."

Father Hesburgh stands and turns to view the campus, but he seems to be looking at more distant horizons. "I'm not worried about the Catholic school system as a system. The life and death problem is to transmit the faith. You know the Jewish people and others have been able to do this for centuries without any elaborate school system. It is really a very personal problem. The worse thing is that the inaction of elders comes to try the faith of young people. We have had a lot of that happen. That's when leadership becomes unavailable. All the problems we are having right now may well get us back to more fundamental ideas, to a more fundamental vision of the faith. That is what we need, a great vision of the sweep of mankind and an understanding that we are just in the middle of the story, that it is a story far from ended, and that we have to contribute our part to keep it moving upward and outward . . ."

EUGENE MCCARTHY

Eugene McCarthy, the former Minnesota Senator and presidential candidate, strikes you as taller, more powerful, and more handsome than televised images have ever made him. He seems to fill the room and yet not be quite present, reminding you of the vigorous young Franklin D. Roosevelt minus the nose-glasses and the guile. McCarthy seems too unaffected to be political, a man persisting in thinking his own thoughts even as the curious world gazes intently at him. We met in his twenty-eighth-floor office in New York's Rockefeller Center where he works as an editor for the publishing house of Simon and Schuster. The gentle mist and rain outside provide a soft contrast for his familiar profile. He points his dark-rimmed glasses to a book review that is spread out on his desk and shakes his head. It is a review of Wilfrid Sheed's book on a composite Irish-Catholic politician, and the reviewer has chosen to incorporate some critical references about McCarthy in his observations.

"That man doesn't even know me," the former Senator says in a subdued voice that has a hard edge on it. "He's just making up that stuff. That's when I begin to wonder if we should defend the freedom of the press or not." He smiles a little tightly and one can sense the constant vulnerability of a celebrity's life space. "That's irresponsible, to write about me without ever having met me. If I had somebody like that on my own staff, I'd get rid of him," McCarthy says firmly. "You can't just make up things about people and call it journalism or an author's freedom." He pushes the review aside, although it is obvious that it is not something that is easy for him to forget. He is a sensitive man, a poet, who, despite his years in public life, has never

grown barnacles on his tenderness. Mystery trails Eugene
McCarthy; he has never been the simple and uncomplicated
hero who might have pleased the liberals more. He may
have heard a different drummer but he also hears other
voices and questions which he pauses to reflect on; the public, seeing him silent and meditative at times, finds him uncertain, or perhaps too complicated to build a new Camelot
for him.

McCarthy had thought once about leading his life as
a monk; and the Benedictine Abbey and college that ride
behind a sail-shaped chapel in Collegeville, Minnesota,
have left a mark on his life and his style. His seriousness is
footnoted, however, with humor that is as dry and clear as
his speaking voice. Close up there is something powerfully
attractive about his presence and the reflective—almost de-
tached—way with which he can regard a world of which
he has been so much a part. He speaks somewhat flatly as
though he would let his ideas stand for themselves and not
adorn them with any artificially generated emotion. Statements are underplayed so that you find yourself paying
close attention to what he says in order to catch the meanings that are almost buried in the lower key of his voice.
And there is also something good-natured and quizzical
about his approach to things, as though he were a man
who had his own private reasons for discounting 10 per
cent of life's solemnity; there is a touch of playfulness in
some of his most reflective comments. It is part of his style,
a way of building some distance between himself and his
observations so that they can seem to move along with an
energy of their own.

"The basic problem of life is a theological one; what's it
all about? I suppose for the Catholic Church in recent
years the question has been to straighten out its forms so that
it could get back to its substance. So many of these accidentals get in people's way in questions of belief. I remember when my daughter Margaret was about seven years of
age and the priest explained that there were really not

three Wise Men at the birth of Jesus, she said"—and he flashes what somebody recognized long ago as a marvelous campaign smile—"at supper that evening now she could understand why Catholics leave the Church." He pauses a moment, recalling that long gone moment and continues, "In faith, however, you have to eliminate what you don't believe in. The problem is why we don't face up to what is left."

McCarthy stretches his arms and, observing that there have been too many books on Catholic nostalgia of late, reflects for a few moments on the contradictions that were involved in so many of the accidentals of Catholic asceticism. "Take the whole idea of intellectual pride or, in matters of faith, the idea of the will to believe. Those things are just contradictions in themselves. But there was some wonderful kind of formulation for everything. I think all of that made it difficult to see and understand the substance of faith. Right now I think we are moving past all of that, moving into new territory. We are coming to what I think the theology of hope is all about. There are many people doing this these days. There is something religious, I think, in what Norman Mailer is trying to do in his writing and thinking these days. He is moving into unknown territory and trying to make some sense out of our experience. I think in some way, in order to do this, we all have to be non-believers of a sort, willing to question and investigate and not be surprised at what we find . . .

"It is like poetry. A poem, somebody once said, is always an accident. Poetry is without freedom; that is no shocking thing for poets to understand. There is some parallel for this in the readiness that we need at the present time to explore our faith." He pauses again, as though distracting himself, and does in fact switch the subject, free associating as a poet at ease might do. "I don't know what you do for sacraments now. There is something poetic about that whole idea with their social and symbolic meaning for our lives. I think that in the Church by trying to make more out of them they've made less out of them." He stops himself again, or so it seems, and now, with a twist of humor, puts the subject aside, as though he had discovered there was no poetry in it after all. "Take Extreme Unction. It is not a sacrament for those who are dying but now for those who are sick. Well, maybe we ought to give Extreme Unction when you get your first social security check. That marks the biggest shift most people will be making at that time in their life." He smiles somewhat diffidently, as though to look away from his own wit. He begins to speak of the Church again. It is clear that he has great affection for it even when he knows intimately its problems and its self-delusions.

"I remember the beginning of the Second Vatican Council and how enthused everyone was about what a wonderful thing it was going to be. I was in Minnesota with President Kennedy just before it began and we went to church in the Cathedral. Whoever it was that gave the homily that day was leaving for Rome to attend the Council and his whole theme was, 'How good it is to go to a council when the Church is not in trouble.'" McCarthy chuckles a bit at the preacher's recollected naïveté, "President Kennedy leaned over to me as the preacher was warming to this theme and said, 'If my organization was in such good shape, I wouldn't have the meeting.'" McCarthy laughs and then his face becomes serious once more. "I think faith alerts us to the redemptive function in life, how we are involved in carrying it out. Chardin gives us a feeling for this, some sense of our responsibility to save society. I am not sure anybody has given us a clear idea of the mystery of good and evil. I think Chardin's ideas are as good as anybody's. It's like saying if you were God what would be the worst thing you could do. Suppose the answer would be to will to be non-being. I think maybe we are on the way back from that toward a fullness of being to be realized in the universe. It is not really creation, but re-creation. I think that is better than Adam and Eve as a theory; that tells us something of where we are and where we are going, and it is a great and difficult mystery. We have to have some sense of this overall process of which we are all a part.

"Then there is a place for institutional Churches, of course. You can't have everybody just be their own institution. I think one of the problems that priests have had is that they have had to look on themselves as double agents; they've had the role of the ancient priests who said, 'I represent the people,' but also the other side of it where they say, 'I represent God.' Of course that last part is rather easy duty . . ." McCarthy's voice trails off. He is not going to explain any more than he has to; he is indeed speaking like a poet who invites you to find his meaning or whatever meaning you can in the statements he throws out. There is something in his tone, however, that speaks to me of some frustration and pain at Churches that have never questioned old formulas and have failed to sense the questions and confusions of contemporary men and women.

"I think there is a call for a new sense of priesthood in the world, one that requires the participation of all of us, one that is freed from this higher level trap where so many priests and bishops have found themselves. They're caught in another world. It is like watching the bishops file into the Vatican Council." McCarthy will give an image, a poet's view of what he sees in the higher clergy and their ceremonics. "I mean they're all persons, they're all intelligent, and there they are wearing these purple robes and cinctures made out of sheepskins or something else. I found a poem about that when I was at the consecration of Paul Moore, the Episcopal Bishop of New York. It was right there on the program. All I had to do was add a last line."

McCarthy goes over to a bookshelf and takes down a volume of his own poetry. He flattens it on his knee and reads in the voice of a man who is obviously asking whether you can sense what he does about the unknowing staidness of so many churchmen. He reads:

The Program
  "The Cross of New York
  The Bishop of New York
        attended by the Coadjutor and the Suffragan
  The Canons of the Cathedral Church

  A Cross
  The Bishops in their order

  The Choir

  A Cross
  The Chancellor and the President
        of the Standing Committee
  The Standing Committee
  The Trustees of the Cathedral
  The Officers of the Diocese
  The Representatives of other Religious Bodies
        and Academic Institutions.
  The Clergy of the Diocese
  The Clergy of other Dioceses
  The Members of Religious Orders
  The Seminarians of the Diocese."

The Instruction

  "The Processions will retire in direct Seniority,
        proceeding the length of the Cathedral,
        and leaving by the Great Bronze Doors."

McCarthy pauses and looks up at me and says, "All I have to
    add is this,"

The Action

            and so they did go
            with dignity
            out through the Great Bronze Doors
            to Amsterdam Avenue.[1]

  [1] "Recessional," from *Other Things and the Aardvark* (Garden City:
Doubleday & Company, Inc., 1970).

"It was right there on the program all the while and as the ceremony went on and on I suddenly realized it. It does say something, I think," but he underplays the last line. You will have to seek out the rest of the meaning for yourself.

I ask him about the meaning of religious activity in the modern world. He still has the book of poetry on his knees as he says, "I think it's related to a sense of obligation to everything and everyone around you. To the extent that Christianity helps to define that, it is a helpful body of religious thought. That is what its task is, but it must continually re-examine itself if it is going to carry this out properly. Take the sacraments again. You have to weigh their social need now against what it was in a different culture and at a different time. That may need to be re-thought right now . . .

"Marriage is a good example. It had an old social function, but maybe it has a new one now. The problem with a sacrament is that it cannot lie about what is really going on in the lives of people and hope to make sense to the world. Then the ritual becomes an anachronism and it does harm. It becomes destructive." McCarthy does not become personal, but it is clear that he feels quite keenly on the subject which he is now discussing. He looks steadily into my eyes.

"Young people's marriage forms capture something of their commitment and their capacity for it. When the forms are way off here or way off there, then it may be better not to have it. I think that it is very difficult for the Church to understand the complexities of what goes on between human beings. When it oversimplifies it in its demands or in its ritual I think it is showing that it really does not under-stand or can't keep up with it. I think that becomes a very bad thing . . ."

He pauses, as a man might who is thinking of whether he wants to say more on this subject or not. He shifts instead to another sacrament. "Confirmation is another thing that can be false to our experience. There is probably a place for this, for noting the time when an individual should take on mature responsibilities, but it is certainly not when you're eleven. I am afraid the Church has it then to make sure to get you before you get out of grade school. I think Baptism and Communion are of a different order than this: they are clearer." McCarthy is saying, in effect, that the Church's language does not match his experience or that of many people he knows in the world. "I think we make it worse when we do things like lifting the interdict we had once placed on Galileo or when that Dominican who was burned at the stake was publicly forgiven in Rome a few years ago. That just makes us look worse. It was bad enough to do it in the first place. But then to seem self-satisfied about forgiving them five hundred years later is a little too much. The world is changing very rapidly and older people do have a great deal of difficulty and understanding that there are new ways of looking at things.

"My son Michael is at Harvard and does a lot of photography. One day an older man said to him, 'You never use the vertical frame.' And Michael answered, 'We don't think that way.' He hadn't really thought about it, but it does illustrate that the way older people have looked at things is just not the way younger people may be looking at them. This may be a kind of an over-simplification, but there's something the Church has to learn from it.

"I think the Church's attitude for too long was this: We know something you don't know. I remember not too many years ago when one of my children was in high school and there was some question about the kind of religion that was being taught out there. I was asked to be on a panel that was discussing this. I took the catechism and read the definition on the first page which said, 'A mystery is a truth which cannot be explained.' Then I turned to page thirty where there was an explanation of the mystery of the Trinity. This kind of lack of logic never strikes these teachers. It's the kind of attitude you can have if you want to deny time and change. It is the very kind of thing that the Church really cannot do anymore with educated and sensitive people. That's doing something wrong to man . . .

"The thing is that religious people did believe everything they were told. There was a time when they didn't care about the logic. Now, as they look back, I think it's quite understandable that many of them say to themselves, 'Either I've been stupid or there's been something fraudulent here.' Take the simple things that were so much a part of Catholic practice, like the nine First Fridays. I suppose if you did it twice, you really had nothing to worry about, unless"—and he smiles broadly—"they canceled each other out . . ."

"I think the Church has to reflect on some big conception of what creation is about. What is the movement of creation? This is where I think it has to deal with this theology of hope. That also applies to our human relationships, to these things that can become so complex between all of us. We start speaking about this priesthood we all share and the obligation we have to other people. That's something that can be informal or formalized. When you formalize it then you can go on to the question of special symbols and so forth, but if you haven't dealt with these deeper questions, then the symbols won't even be appropriate . . .

"And there's the whole question of history and what it tells us of the past and how it helps us to deal with the present. We should have learned something from the episodes of Galileo and others. We have to learn that it is perfectly all right to ask questions, that this is an important part of believing: to ask the right questions about yourself and the world you live in. I think it is a terrible thing when the Church cannot keep up with people when they are asking the questions that need to be placed at the present time."

It is clear that McCarthy is a man who writes questions as he does poetry, who cannot prevent them from rising in his consciousness by any act of the will. There is almost a touch of longing in his voice, as though he really wished that there could be a Church sensitive enough to let men question what they cannot understand before it censures them for some failure in belief. But he turns aside from this theme as though he were pulling back from something he felt very personally and that he must use some humor to set the conversation into proper perspective again.

"Celibacy is really better for politicians than for the clergy in their role in society today, I don't have any doubts about that. I think that birth control and abortion are pretty tough propositions. They require a lot of thought. You know I really thought we lost birth control in the Congo when some bishop said that the nuns could take birth control pills if they were afraid they were going to be raped. Well what happens to all the natural law arguments if you can make that kind of an exception? And I wonder about many of the unanswered questions connected with abortion. There were many old theological opinions about the viability of the fetus. They made distinctions about whether the fetus should be baptized or not, but they used an arbitrary number of days, forty or ninety or something like that. Once you make those kinds of distinctions, it does something to the absolute tone which they use in other sides of the argument. What about all the theologians who said that you could abridge the right of the mother to life if the baby could be saved? Isn't her life just as sacred as that of the infant's? That leaves you asking, 'Well, where do we go from here?' I don't think we can be afraid of the questions connected with all these issues, and we certainly cannot pretend that they do not exist . . ."

I turn the question to politics and to his own conception of his role in 1968, asking whether or not he perceived it as possessing religious significance. He does not answer right away, but with the voice of a man who has thought a lot about these questions, he goes on. "Well I thought we did have something going, a real movement. I think we had a constituency of conscience. Then we were saying to the country that we had problems that were serious and that we had to approach and deal with. Now I think George McGovern was almost a pure Methodist preacher in the way he approached the American people. He didn't have that context of meaning I think is important. He was asking the people to be against something, to make a moral judgment on somebody else. The country didn't respond and the reason was simple. They didn't want to make judgments on themselves.

"In 1968 we didn't want to make judgments on Lyndon; we were not interested in imputing moral fault to him. That wasn't the issue. When people get into these positions of power the conditions that affect them make them see the world very differently. It's like ITT. Those people live in another country, and once in a while they come out and see the way the rest of us have to live. You can't be believable without the right context. I think that is really what George didn't have. I met a young man recently in an airport. It was almost like something out of the Old Testament. He said to me, and this was before the election, 'Nixon will win. The people won't vote against their own guilt.' You know, that was a remarkable statement. I almost expected to see the young man depart in a chariot into the skies, as though his life had been justified by that insight. McGovern didn't offer the people any salvation, just condemnation. But Nixon said something like, 'I'm okay. You're okay. We're guilty together.' But he never moved beyond that. While he was saying that, McGovern kept telling the people they were all guilty. Nobody in that campaign offered pardon or any clear and decent way of salvation. I think the people could have been moved; they could have been helped to understand the issues such as those on poverty, or individual liberties, or the other things that are really at the heart of life. I think that is what we tried to offer, a context that gave us a clear way of dealing with our problems, admitting them, and of finding some kind of real salvation through changing ourselves." He does not seem harsh or bitter, but it is clear that he feels he did something purposeful and honest, something he believed in and something he feels made him a believable candidate.

"We're all defining our meaning all the time. We're en-

gaged, as some philosopher said, in a revolt against the unbelievable and against irrelevance. But somehow we've got
to get these issues into perspective so that people can recognize them as genuinely religious. We have to work it down
where it reaches the people who don't go to Church anymore; somehow it's got to be reduced to their level.

"I think the young people do have an idea about a priesthood of service, that they want to do something to help the
rest of the world. They're really looking for leadership,
for somebody to show them how to do that effectively. The
young sense that they don't know what they want to happen; the tragedy is that they don't feel they could make it
happen even if they did know. They don't have any representation, and they feel that there are forces they cannot
influence that are directing their lives. We need somebody
to represent this kind of impulse. It's not the same kind of
thing that George Wallace said, although he came closest,
I suppose, to try to speak for the average man. He said,
in effect, that he really didn't represent people but that he
would take care of them. He said, 'I won't let them bother
you; I won't let them bust your children, tax your house, or
send your boys to war.'"

McCarthy pauses again, thinking of what? He shrugs and
goes on, "I think we need somebody to represent our deeper
aspirations in a clearer and less selfish way. I think that
Moltmann in his *Theology of Hope* said it up to the point
we are now, to the point where it had to be said. We're
really the ones who have to carry it on." He turns back to
his own political vision for a moment. "We tried to offer
a way of redeeming society, to let America admit that it
had been wrong and that we have to pay more attention
to the poor and that we have to care about individual lib-
erty. I think that it is a religious thing, that is the kind of
thing that gives hope. I just don't think you can divide
these things . . ."

The subject shifts to prayer, and after being interrupted
by a brief phone call, McCarthy goes on. "I don't know

how you define prayer. I suppose it is saying, 'Here I am,' and letting yourself have a chance to reflect on life and on God. I always thought Vespers was a pretty good thing for that. There was incense and there was a pretty good mood to it; it was at the right time of day in the evening with no pressure connected with it. Every other religious service had to have some other special intention and Vespers just wasn't loaded down with this. It had something of the freedom of the dance in it, especially at solemn Vespers." The poet is obviously speaking again, with prayerful times remembered that can no longer be found in a crowded and noisy world, "And, of course, you don't have Vespers any-where anymore."

I ask him whether being a poet did not make a person stand on the front lines as some kind of a man of prayer at this time in history. He picks up the book of poetry from which he had read before and, smiling gently at a thought that he likes but would have hesitated to say for himself, he says, "I wrote a preface for this book that may have something to say about what we've been talking about. It goes like this:

"The ancient map makers used the term *terra terribilia* to identify what was beyond their knowledge of the earth. A notation on one of these maps describe the *terra terribilia* in these words:

> All beyond is nothing
> but dry and desert sands,
> inhabited only by wild creatures
> or dark impassable bogs,
> of Scythian cold
> or frozen sea,
> beyond which there is nothing
> but monstrous and tragical fiction.
> There the poets
> and inventors of fables dwell.[2]

[2] From the Preface to *Other Things and the Aardvark.*

"I wrote that book as a tribute to American poets, for men like Robert Lowell, William Stafford, Reed Wittemore, James Dickey, Philip Booth, and the many others who have written of this country and of its people. These poets have gone beyond the 'known' and the 'certain' into the *terra terribilia* in the search for truth."

That is where McCarthy stands, a believer who, in his own way, will always be trying to find the path into the dark forest that surrounds the modern world.

I never understood the Jewish women of the Old Testament until I got to know Ann Landers, "Eppie" as she is called by anyone who knows her well. There is no confusion in her mind between her famous writing name as an advice columnist, Ann Landers, and her own identity as Mrs. Jules Lederer. When you are with her you sense a combination of energy and intelligence, of sharp-wittedness and purpose that makes her one of the most interesting and attractive women I have ever met. Pretense is an alien thought to her and I know few healthier sounds than that of her spontaneous laughter.

When I meet her she is eager to talk about the subject of believing, anxious to think about the subject out loud with the same gusto with which she attacks most other problems in life. We look out of her fifteenth-floor apartment at the view of Lake Shore Drive trailing off into the foggy distance. Some coffee and cakes are served and she begins. "Faith is an unconditional and unquestioning confidence in somebody or something. It is not looking for accurate evidence of proof. That doesn't go along with it. Faith required a trust that is completely given. Now you know"—and Eppie sips some coffee and pauses briefly—"experience is the most important ingredient in this. If people disappoint, if they are not honest, if they are not genuine, if they break something that has been said in confidence, then I lose faith in them; then I can no longer believe.

"Faith is a very enriching thing in life. It has meaning at different levels. A lot of people don't have it. They don't believe in themselves. A lot of people believe in me, I know that. They have a feeling that I'm on the level and I protect that faith; I work hard to protect that because I sense what it means for people to put their faith in what I say. I try to learn, find out from experts what I don't know, and work hard at what I'm doing. In other words," she continues with the practical tone that has made her famous, "I deliver. That gives me faith in myself, and I believe in me and others can believe in me. That's the way it works."

What of religious faith? I ask. "Religious faith is not the same as the faith I have in myself and others. It used to be something instilled even before a person reached the age of reason; much of what we call religious faith is what has been installed before the age of reason. It is deeply rooted in the early part of life. I think this is particularly true of Catholics who seem to have many difficulties with fear and guilt. The person who grows up and is genuinely faithful in religion is that way because he started early at it. Sometimes something can jar them into a kind of religious faith later on. They make a deal with God over some illness or a need for a job or something. I am afraid that is the way a lot of religious faith develops. A strain of infantilism runs through the faith of many people. There are certainly people who have a fairly mature religious faith, but there are a lot who have a case of arrested development. They are stuck at about the sixth-year level. I am afraid that this is the faith we see most often. It is connected with the punishing ideas of that old-time religion. You have to behave. If you don't, you'll get punished, you'll be unpleasing in the eyes of God. My biggest complaint about the Church is that it has taught people the religious faith that is so filled with fear."

What, then, would be the characteristics of a mature faith? Eppie shifts for just a moment in her chair and says thoughtfully, "It is to have had some very rough knocks, some dirty deals in life, and then to believe in God anyway. It is to face all these things and say to yourself that this is not punishment, bad luck, or the way the mop flopped. With mature faith we are able to believe in the goodness of God and the goodness of man and sometimes because of the tragedies we have to face. Mature faith believes despite the evidence that God does not exist. I'll give you a good example," and Eppie smiles, before going on. "Hubert Humphrey is a man of faith. He has had more devastating disappointments in his life than anybody I know. He lost the presidency by an eyelash; why he even has a retarded grandchild. That man has an incredible capacity to forgive and to bounce back into life again. The trouble is people sometimes get the wrong idea about Hubert. They speak about Hubert the joke or Hubert the potato head, and he is not that way at all. He's a lovely spirit, a genuinely good man.

"I don't think that a person ought to waste his time on small fights. They take up too much of your energy. You have to conserve your energy for what you're trying to do in life. Hating eats up energy quicker than anything I know. That's what I admire about Hubert. He has never wasted his time on petty things . . ."

Eppie pours me another cup of coffee and, without the stimulus of a question, goes on. "I believe in a good God. Incidentally," as she looks directly at me, "my belief in God is somewhat infantile. I think he is loving and all protecting because he has loved and protected me. This is a very personal thing. I talk to him all the time. Like Tevye in *Fiddler on the Roof*. I call God up like I call anybody up, and his line is never busy.

"I'm very suspicious about pat answers about belief. Man is fundamentally good and I think he wants to do good. All persons start out good. I really don't believe in original sin. Something happens in their early years to damage them. An unloving child is not born, he is made. That damage is very hard to shake in life. Parental rejection causes most of the trouble. That's one of the reasons I am liberal about abortion. I think that we have killed too many people after they have been born. Yes, the people who are close to us as we are growing up can do a great deal of damage, and that affects the way a person believes." Eppie thinks for a moment and, obviously a woman who has never let life just happen to her, interrupts herself, "Now there comes a point in any life, no matter how much trouble a person has had, where he has to say, 'Enough of this! Now I'm going to do something about my problems.' That's very important. People may not be able to solve them completely, but they can almost always do something constructive about them.

"I think feeling too sorry for ourselves is one of the big sins we can commit in life. Of course the sins of omission are serious, and those are connected with faith, with failing to believe in each other. The biggest sin of omission is not coming through for somebody who loves you; that's a bigger sin than doing something ugly. It's a sin to fail to give love, affection, and gratitude at the moments when they are most needed in the lives of those close to us. The big sin is failing to be there when somebody needs you. The sinners are all around us. They are the people who cop out when they are really needed. They do most of the emotional damage in life. One of the big parts of believing is continuing to believe in people when they are in trouble. I am thinking of a friend of mine who has gone through some terrible things with a child who went wrong and got into drugs. Suppose somebody else has had a stinking divorce. These are the things that really hurt people's hearts. When they get into the middle of these things that's when they find themselves pretty much alone. People turn away and, in effect, say to them that they don't care. Believing in people means that we are ready to give them emotional support. They need understanding and acceptance at these times, and they can only get it from us."

Eppie speaks with strong feeling as she chooses an example from the morning's newspaper story that Federal Judge Otto Kerner has been found guilty of profiting from an inside stock deal during his term as Governor of Illinois. "Even in the trial of Otto Kerner, well, my heart aches for him. There were lots of people who used to nuzzle up to him and they won't do it anymore. That's because he can't help them anymore and because he is disgraced for life by what's happened. The worst of it is the rejection he is going to face for the rest of his life. I don't know him that well, but I feel very intensely for him. You have to stick with people. You have to come through for them. That's what I try to tell people to do, to come through for each other.

"The people in my life that I believe in and care about I want to be first class. I want them to behave in a first-class way, particularly younger people. A friend of mine who is a freshman in college started as an art major. When I went to a Braque exhibit I bought a catalogue and sent it to her. For two months I didn't hear anything. Then a few weeks ago I was in the city where she lives and I met her again. She said, 'I apologize for not writing,' but I said, 'Well if your mother hadn't told me that you had gotten the catalogue, I would never have known it. I'm not going to say it's okay. If I wasn't too busy to get it for you, you shouldn't have been too busy not to write. You have to do things right. I expect to hear from you.' When I got home I had a letter from her, thanking me for not letting her off the hook. She said that my scolding had been a great compliment. She thought that I really cared.

"I have faith in what people can be," and her tone tightens to match her urgent mood, "and I really push them. I want them to be their best selves. That college girl was not her best self, but that's one of the things I really believe in—bringing that out in people. I needle and nag them," describes the way she keeps after people to do their best. "It's an amazing thing," she says with a smile. "I have a mind like a steel trap and a memory like an elephant. That is one of the best things about never drinking. You remember everything that has taken place during the evening. A lot of other people don't. I am also very hard on myself in this regard. If I say that I am going to do something, then I do it. I believe in coming through. To come through for others means that you say what you mean, you mean what you say, and then you deliver the goods. That's faith in a practical way.

"I want people to have faith in me. I work hard at keeping the faith, baby," and she laughs her infectious laugh. "I'm very sensitive about the name Ann Landers. I wouldn't commercialize it for anything. You know, on my radio show, if I were willing to read a commercial my salary would double. I won't do it. I'm willing to pay in that practical way to preserve people's faith in me. I have had fabulous offers to mention products. That's what I call protecting people's faith in me. As soon as I sell something, I'm finished. But, to get back to what we were saying, keeping faith means to be there with people when they need you."

What, I ask, would she like her grandchildren to believe in? "First of all, I would like them to believe in themselves, to have a good opinion of themselves. Secondly, I want them to believe in other people. They simply are not going to be able to do that unless they believe in themselves. And above all that, I want them to believe in God. It is wonderful to watch them taking turns saying grace before meals. They seem to have an easy relationship, they find it easy to talk to God in those simple moments."

I ask her if she has ever felt any kinship with the Jewish women of the Old Testament. She laughs uproariously at my suggestion but says seriously, "I am sure that my faith comes from the old Jewish tradition. I grew up with no feelings of sin or guilt. That's an important part of my calm and quiet center. Sometimes I've been ashamed if I didn't live up to my best self. Sometimes I feel I have disappointed God, but I never felt that I let him down seriously and he has never let me down. By the way," and she laughs again, "God is Jewish, I want you to remember that.

"But you've had some good people. Now John XXIII was my kind of pope. There was a great human being. There was the kind of religious leader that people could believe in. You could really believe in him. It's from men like that that we learn what faith is all about."

I question her about a theory she has previously told me
that all the good people in the world finally get to meet each
other. She laughs again but adds, "It's true, it really is true.
When I meet somebody with ideas I respect I always find
out that we already have many of the same friends. There is
a network of people who respond to each other. They
seem to believe and live by the same thing.

"We have to peg people to put them in certain slots by
what they believe in. You know if I met someone with a
high regard for the late Joe McCarthy, I could put them in
a slot. Or how about the people who say, 'Everybody on
welfare is a bum,' or 'The blacks are pushing too fast,' or
'We had colored help and treated them like the family.' I love
that last one. I always ask those people, 'You mean they ate
with you?' The minute a phony comes on my radar screen
all the lights go red. Unmasking phonies is one of my
specialties." And, with a tone of mischief, she adds, "I've
got *Chutzpah*. That means guts. It takes that to do some of
the unmasking that I do with other people," and she goes
on to tell a story that casts her in an Old Testament role
perfectly. "Well, I guess I did challenge a General once. It
was Westmoreland in 1967. It was in May and I was on a
tour of Vietnam and I challenged him about the war. I told
him it was immoral and unwinnable. That's what I mean
about coming through about what you believe in. What we
do has consequences. You either have to put up or shut up
when you have the chance. If you're in a position to do
something and you don't do it, then I can't have faith in you.
I just could not have believed in myself if I had walked out
of his office and not told him what I thought. I would have
felt unfaithful to myself. I told him everything I felt and
that was pretty early to be against the war. I said it was
tearing the country apart and that we were not going to win
the war." She interrupts herself, "By the way I didn't appreciate Father Philip Berrigan calling the prisoners of war,
'war criminals.' I am sure there is enough guilt already about
this war without adding any to it now."

Checking her watch, she notes that she must be getting down to her office. Would I care to walk along with her? As we get ourselves together she continues talking, "My idea of hell would be to have opportunities to do good and not to be able to respond to them, or to leave unfinished the things you might have done. Seeing things through is a very important dimension of life and maturity.

"I also believe in walking," she says, and soon we are on East Lake Shore Drive bucking the famous Chicago wind. As we move swiftly along I ask her about something closely connected with faith, the subject of fidelity. "Fidelity is a vanishing virtue, I am afraid. One third of the women are working; you know men and women who work together get to play together. And sometimes those who pray together play together. I am not so sure there is anything wrong with that. I knew a pastor years ago, a handsome man who was running a little to fat when I got to know him, and I noticed his housekeeper moved with him from parish to parish . . ." She looks at me, bright-eyed, and laughs heartily. She is in a playful mood—enjoying the walk, the bracing cold air, and the chance to make a few more observations on the human situation which she has known so well in her years as an advice columnist.

"What," I ask her, "keeps most people together?" "Damn little!" she says, roaring with laughter.

"Well, how do most couples get along?" I ask. "Rotten! They have a hard time of it. That's how faith is tested. It's tested by life all the time. That's where it works, when they have to face and work through things together."

"Why do people stick together?" I ask. "Fear!" she exclaims, laughing again. "Seriously, though, faith is really under the test at close quarters between people. They have to have it if they are going to stick together. There is something about man and woman at the bottom of it all. That's one of the great experiences of life. It tests our faith but it helps us to understand it too. That's where we begin to realize what things are all about." We are at the Sun Times

Building in a few moments. As we part company Eppie is still laughing at the foibles we all share in the human condition. "Keep the faith," she calls, stepping on the escalator that will take her to the office where she keeps faith with her millions of readers.

DALE FRANCIS

The old America of small towns with lush green hills just outside their city limits may still be found in the heartland of Indiana. It is not surprising that the quiet county seat town of Huntington should be the home for the moderately conservative *National Catholic Register* and its editor, convert to Catholicism, Dale Francis. The *Register*'s offices are on the fourth floor of the La Fontaine Hotel, an ancient brick structure struggling to maintain a well-scrubbed face in the downtown area where relatively new one-way streets give the only hint of metropolitan woes. Dale Francis, with the benign features of a gentle Charles Laughton, greets me in his simple, book-crammed office where he writes and assembles each week's edition of the 90,000-circulation paper. Dressed in an open-neck blue sport shirt, he talks briefly about the newspaper, the main framework of which is used in many dioceses where a local Catholic paper is not a possibility.

"When I took over there was an editor and eleven assistants, and they were losing money. Now there is just me and two assistants. This is my fourth year of doing it; I do most of the writing in here and I enjoy it." He sounds like a man who likes to work, in his own way, in an office where he is virtually a one-man staff. "I came off a daily paper, so getting this together is not so bad. What is difficult today is knowing exactly what to say or how to choose your news stories. Editing a Catholic newspaper used to be comparatively simple. It's not so easy anymore. You know when I was in North Carolina we went right after the race issue.

That wasn't easy to do down there. We don't have those simple, direct things to do in the same way anymore."

I ask him about the nature of believing and what he thinks it involves. "I don't know. I simply believe very much in God, in Christ as the Incarnation, and in the Catholic Church as the Church he founded. From this everything else follows." Francis speaks in a quiet, gentle voice. It is hard to imagine that it is ever raised very much out of anger or impatience. What part of the person is involved in believing? I ask him, as he moves to a chair on the same side of the desk with me. "The whole of myself is involved in believing. My belief is in no way a compartment of my life. It's . . . it's"—and he speaks very softly now—"the direction of my whole life. It has been as long as I remember, and that goes back long before I was a Catholic. I have a feeling that people have different capacities for belief. It has not been possible for me since I was four or five not to have belief in God directing my life. I have never had a time in my life without belief. I can remember a time and a place when I was about five years old when I began thinking seriously about God. That has been a directing part of everything I have ever done." He smiles, as in a pleasant recollection, "The first thing I ever had published was a poem about Christ."

Francis shifts in his chair; he is looking inward, rather than at me. "From my first memories—I have a gift of almost total recall; I am sure I am the only one from my fourth grade class in Troy, Ohio, who can tell you the seating arrangement—until I became a Catholic I had a sense of incompletion. That was not dissatisfaction. I didn't have that. It was rather an unsatisfaction. When I finally became a Catholic I had a sense of 'Here I was'—a sense of completion. Before that I always knew I just wasn't where I was ultimately supposed to be. Belief for me is all of a piece. It surely is. It didn't change when I became a Catholic. I was never dissatisfied where I was. I served as a Methodist pastor for four years. What I felt was a kind of movement toward a destination."

I ask him to describe this further. "Well, it's kind of placing yourself in a rhythm of God. I try to keep an open prayer life, an open communication with God. I have said very few prayers ever asking for anything in my life. But ever since I was a little child I have kept a consciousness of God. There is something more prayer about that than the things we call prayer. It's in the line of experiencing God. This is something that is hard to describe. You simply have to feel that you are in harmony with God. There are things I have never written—things I prefer not to write—about where I can see God has worked in my life."

He gets up and moves across the room to turn off the noisy air conditioner, and taking his chair again, begins. "In 1946 Bishop Waters asked me to come to North Carolina. That time"—and Francis hesitates for just a moment—"I said to myself, 'From now on I commit myself totally to what God wants me to do.' And since that time I have gone to places I have never dreamed of or never thought I would go to. It all comes simply from putting myself in God's hands and trying to discern Providence in my daily life. I have seen it so many times move me. When you can place yourself in God's hands it just works that way. I always ask for guidance from the Holy Spirit." He pauses because he wants to make something clear, "Now it is not my nature to be emotional about the Spirit. That's just not my way, but I do try to seek the guidance of the Spirit. I think that is an absolute necessity. When I try to figure things out too carefully for myself they simply don't go nearly as well as when I trust to Providence." Francis pauses a moment. "You know I wanted to go to Spain with my first wife after we knew she had a terminal illness, but we wound up going to Cuba. My mother had within that previous year been killed in an automobile accident, and my father had come down with cancer as had my wife's father. Well, all that changed our plans a lot. We packed everything we had, and when we came to a little town in Cuba I said, "Here's where we're going to live. It was San Miguel De Los Baños and two blocks away the Cardinal had a little summer home and I got to know the newspaper people down there and many other wonderful people. Everything opened up to us. We got to know almost all the persons who were doing things in Cuba. It was one of the great experiences of my life. Every time we had to move, as in going back to Texas after that, we tried to go along with Providence. It was the same way when I had planned to do graduate studies at Yale and yet, suddenly two weeks before I was to go there, I switched to Notre Dame. You just have to do things that feel right in the Spirit. You have to catch the winds right. I really think there is a lot in what Satchel Paige had to say. That is good solid advice. 'Stay loose and don't look back.' "

Francis stirs in his chair a moment. "We've had a lot of sad things in life. My son is brain injured and retarded, and yet he has been a great joy in many ways. It wasn't traumatic. It didn't give us that kind of trouble. We have always tried to see things in terms of faith, and we have been able to accept things. My first wife, Barbara, had a great simplicity. She made great use of her last illness. She was a writer, and although she was ill for nine years, in every way she tried to help other people and she never let herself be an invalid." He smiles again in recollection, a sad but happy smile. "She even chose the funeral home before she died, a Mexican-American place. That was just never heard of in the southwest, but she thought that it might help them get some more Anglo customers." Francis strokes his chin as he continues his reflections. "We have had some powerful experiences, but I wouldn't call any of them difficult experiences. We didn't sense any of them that way. At no time have they ever pressed hard. That's a fact. That doesn't seem logical, but it is a fact. As for Barbara, seeing her in pain was very difficult. It was difficult for her knowing that she was going to die, but it never brought us down. It wasn't that we had to turn to faith for consolation. Faith was just there. We have never had to turn to it because it is simply a part of everything we have done.

"After Barbara's death I knew I would never marry again, mostly because loving carries so much pain with it. Barbara left word with four different friends to tell me that she hoped I would marry again, however. And I came to know I needed to get married again. The one thing I didn't want to do was to get into the dating game and all of that. I thought of the people I had known; I thought of a young lady that both Barbara and I had known and whom I hadn't seen in eight or nine years. We dined, corresponded, and gradually discovered our love for each other. Some men are fortunate to have one good wife; I have had two. We've been married for eleven years, and Margaret has that same wonderful simplicity of faith. In both my marriages faith has been very important. I have never had a sense in marriage of anything but oneness, never a sense of two people. I know that sounds corny. I just don't think we have a sense of two people trying to adjust as much as a sense of living together.

"I think a consciousness of marriage as one sacrament that continues in your life is something important. Anybody who knows us would know this about us. I feel that when I make the coffee for my wife, that's administering the sacrament of matrimony. That vision—that being married is not an event but a continuing experience of a sacrament—is absolutely necessary. You have to work out your living in Christ; and this is the action of the two of you on one another. Since you are each administering a sacrament, you are united in a way that is very remarkable. The only hard things are the illnesses and the suffering. Because you love another you feel great pain when the other has to suffer. When we were in Cuba we saw so many desperately poor people Barbara would say, 'What a wonderful place Cuba would be if you didn't love the people.' The pain they suffer and not being able to do much about it; that is what is hard."

I ask him whether his seemingly very happy life makes it

difficult for him to appreciate that many other people, even people of good will, are unable to live out their marriages in this fashion. He nods his head slowly. "A great many people bring me their problems. I'm not unaware of the fact that people have problems . . ." I ask him about Cuba and Castro since he was there just before the take-over. "Castro made sense in terms of what Batista failed to do. Batista's police started murdering at random, and I did a series of articles on Batista and the people he killed. They were factual articles that were reprinted in many places in the world. I think it had a big effect on the antagonism that grew toward Batista. I spent some time with Castro when he first came in. I visited him with the Archbishop who had saved him from being killed in a previous effort at revolution. I asked him about communism and he said he was opposed to it. My first articles reported that that was what he had said. As a result I was attacked very strongly by the John Birch Society. In fact, a whole issue of the *American Opinion* was written as an open letter to me. It made me sound like a conspirator. Then I went on to write a series of articles showing how Castro was moving Communists into key positions. In Cuba in 1959 it was impossible to make the people think that Castro was turning the government Communist. The Bishops just didn't have the strength to be heard there." I ask him whether bishops are effective in such situations. "Well, there was a survey made in Cuba where the bishops were poor men. The people felt that the Church was identified with the poor. I thought that was a good thing."

I ask him about the nature of the faith in Catholic countries of South and Central America. "Well so many of them say they are Catholics, but then they don't go to Mass. There is something incomplete there. It is not really faith. They think of themselves as Catholics as they think of themselves as Cubans. I think there was a great deal of living of the faith there, however. I know that there are lots of Catholics who are just nominal Catholics. I suppose the faith is pretty thin there. In North Carolina, where Catholics are a minority, you're more likely to find good Catholics practicing."

What of this difficulty of so much belief that seems not to be very deep or committed? "Every Catholic must finally be a convert. There has to be some time after their adult consciousness when what it means to be committed to Christ comes home to them. They have to have some sense of experiential religion. I don't mean the baptism of the Spirit. I don't believe there are two baptisms, and I don't mean John Wesley's sanctification. But that's the direction that's important. People must move from a nominal relationship into an experiential relationship with God. That is what believing is all about.

"A great many Catholics, including priests too, might not understand what this is we're talking about. It is hard to speak about being placed in Christ. It is difficult for people to come to a real realization of this in their lives." I ask him what the faith in practice means to most persons. "I don't know. I certainly see Catholics making decisions I can't understand; I am amazed that Catholics can think that you could be anti-Semitic. How can you have devotion to Mary and be anti-Semitic? I certainly believe Catholics need to involve themselves in social action, but I think that has to follow organically from what you believe in about God and man. There is too much social action from the desire for social action rather than because of the necessary progress associated with religion." I ask him what he means by this and he replies, "It is important to recognize human dignity. That is what is the basis for social action. Then these things follow appropriately."

Why should there be any social action at all? I ask. What is the root motivation for it? "Because you must love your neighbor," he says, "it follows from everything else you believe. You can't very well be a Catholic and hate your neighbor." I observe that many Catholics who look on themselves as good members of the faith have in fact indulged in various forms of prejudice. "Yes, I know that. I have known priests that way too." He pauses for a moment, "I long ago realized that people have different degrees of sensitivity. I accept that."

I offer him an example for comment, saying that I know many priests who do not work hard but who remain in the priesthood and are judged faithful servants, a designation I do not believe they deserve. I also note that many earnest men who have left the priesthood have been deep believers in Christ's message. Francis looks directly back at me and in a thoughtful manner goes on. "I know lots of them, lots of good ones who have left and lots of insensitive ones who have stayed. People are just different. It is hard to judge them, but I have noticed a correlation. The people who get to daily Mass are often those who help other people too. They show concern for them. I suspect that people who come close to some form of tithing would help others too.

"We're not just talking about Catholics. This is a problem for all believers. There aren't that many dedicating their whole lives to people." He is obviously troubled about the issue of social action, however, and he goes on to speak about an old hero of his. "Walter Rauschenbusch of Colgate-Rochester—there was a great influence on many people. He fully loved people. He could never keep a heavy coat; he was always giving them away and he excited Protestantism in the thirties. It was because of him Protestantism was filled with people committed to social Christianity. In his followers' lives it was a kind of humanistic thing, but it came from a man who did what he did out of total belief."

What gets him up in the morning to face each day? "I get up at 5:30 because I like to," he answers with genuine enthusiasm, "because every day is exciting. I really have a kind of excitement about life and about starting each day." He seems so content and at peace that I ask him, "Why are you the man that you are?" And he answers, "My parents, my nature. People differ by nature and I never judge anyone harshly. People do things because of their nature. I know there are others who are not like me. I could never break anything in anger, but a lot of other people could do that and that would be all right. That would be their nature. I think people would get along better if they didn't expect people to act like themselves. It has taken me a long time to realize that: how different we all may be. People have different backgrounds and different ways of looking at things. I used to say—in a way that I'm not sure I would use anymore—that we're made with different God-cavities that we must fill. Some just have a greater tendency to spiritual growth. My prayer life began when I was five, and no one ever taught me to do this. It is simply a part of my nature . . . don't expect all Catholics are going to respond on the same level, but all who understand what the basic Christian message is will certainly have to love their neighbor and do what they can for them."

I ask him about disciplinary regulations in the Church in which, in effect, we demand the same response from everybody. "I have no difficulty in accepting this. I think there is a value in this, as there was in the Friday abstinence from meat. I did that long before I was ever a Catholic as a small sacrifice. I think people doing things together like that has a value in unifying them . . ." What about things more crucial that have divided people in the Church, things like the pope's encyclical on birth control? "*Humanae Vitae?*" he asks, "I'm quite willing to accept the rules laid down for me, assuming there is no conflict with my conscience. I would accept what the pope says. I would have no problem with it." Would you, I ask him, allow freedom to others in this regard? "Well, I would think they weren't understanding the Church as I do as an imperfect people struggling on their way. I think that if the Church splinters, we lose unity and a sense of peace. Now a couple who honestly decide that they must use artificial contraception, I wouldn't judge them harshly. I wouldn't think that it was objectively right, but I wouldn't think that some of the things that theologians have said about this are right either. I heard a noted theologian say recently, without any arguments, that the Holy

Spirit inspired him better than Pope Paul on this question. I think he was very imprudent in saying that . . ."

What do you do with people who disagree in such matters? I ask him. "I don't think we throw them out; although I think they endanger their relationship of being in rhythm with God by these attitudes. This is really an area where I don't do a lot of thinking. What the Church says to do is like an umpire in a ball game. If we're going to have a game, I'll go by that even if I think it is a mistake. I've done that a lot in my life. Well, that's the way it is . . ."

What is important for people to believe in? "What I said in the beginning: in God, Christ as the Incarnation, the Catholic Church as the true Church. Outside of that I can't list anything. Everything else follows from that. Just like the question of celibacy. I recognize it's a rule. I just say it is a rule, and I wouldn't think anything wrong in arguing against it. Believing the Catholic Church is the true Church doesn't make me believe God wants any of these things that are rules in some absolute way, but I accept them. I'd let others fight to change them. Some of the things priests have written about sex seem to me an argument for changing celibacy; some of them are very unrealistic."

What, then, are the things that one must believe in? "I think we have to have belief in the Incarnation and the Resurrection. These are the most vital to me. I think it essential to believe in the Scriptures and in Christ. We have to understand that as we act toward others, we act toward Christ." He pauses for a moment and goes on. "The Virgin birth is a necessity because it is clearly taught in the Scriptures and it is taught by the Church. I have discussed this with many people, and some don't think it's so important. I don't know that it's necessary; I just believe it is true. People who start qualifying the Virgin birth qualify the Incarnation too. The Church has always taught us that it is very important. I don't think the official Church would ever change in this matter. I would be very disturbed if it did.

Too many people in my Protestant experience qualified it and moved on to strange concepts of the Incarnation.

"Nothing that I believed as a Protestant was altered when I became a Catholic. I didn't have to stop believing in anything. There was just a greater fullness. I don't conceptualize things in the way this question is framed. I have never sat down and said these are the things you must believe in. I don't think visions or miracles are so important except that the whole of life is a kind of miracle."

I ask him about current movements in the Church. "I'm concerned about every new movement. I was the first to write about the *Cursillo*, the first to write about the Citizens for Educational Freedom. I'm interested in all of these things. But that doesn't mean I have to get involved. I am interested in seeing what comes and how it develops. I am very open minded about these things. It is very exciting to see things grow in the Church."

Can he specify anything he would call dangers to the faith? "Oh," he says softly, "I don't know. A lot of these things I'm revising my thinking about. I'm a little leery about some of the new language about a sense of community. I think there has been a disintegration about our sense of community among Catholics. I sense that priests don't have the same camaraderie that they used to have. That they have to talk a little while with each other before they find out that they are brothers. Of course, I don't know how deep their camaraderie ever was. I do know that Catholics meeting Catholics used to feel some sense of identity. This at least is gone. Perhaps it was superficial, I don't know."

What of the bishops whom he has supported so strongly in his writings? "Well, I've thought a lot about the bishops lately and a lot about their qualities. You know I read a lot of criticism of them, a lot about their plainness. Generally, however, I think they are the right men. Studying it over about twenty years I have a sense we are getting the right men. I've known insensitive bishops and others who are not the most brilliant men, but I am generally impressed with the

kind of men who have become bishops–especially compared
with the kind who have become bishops in Protestantism. In
Protestantism they are always the most outgoing kind, more
gregarious than in the Catholic Church. The Catholic
Church gets a lot of quiet men who don't stand out. Maybe
that's the best. I can't think of a single bishop that you could
describe as a charismatic leader. I can't think of one. In fact,
I would be a little worried if we had five or six dynamic
charismatic leaders. But my faith tells me that we are getting good bishops and that the Church will continue to
grow . . ."

B. F. SKINNER

Although it is mid-April, the day is crisp and March-like and the scarves on the Harvard students flutter like pennants in the wind. I make my way toward the fifteen-story William James Hall which rises like a modern bank that has unexpectedly found itself anchored in the red brick sea of the university. On the seventh floor are the offices and laboratory of Dr. B. F. Skinner, acknowledged as the most influential of American psychologists and author of the Utopian novel *Walden Two* as well as the recent best seller *Beyond Freedom and Dignity*. The laboratory door is open and, apart from the clatter of the measuring devices which are recording the experimental movements of a brace of pigeons, the room is very quiet. A few young professors and graduate students move along in the special abstraction that sometimes grips these types. A sign, pinned to the door of the laboratory, reads "Will the last one out, please close the door?" The generally subdued atmosphere, except for the pigeons dancing out their strange teletyped messages, is surprisingly banal, especially as one considers the impact of Professor Skinner and his research on the world's imagination.

Dr. Skinner's office has the classic lines and bland paint colors that are the hallmark of contemporary educational buildings. Aside from some photographs of his family and a set of his own books bound in leather on his desk, there is little that seems personal about it; it looks like a place where he stops and sees people rather than a place where he concentrates and works. It is not surprising to hear him say later that he rises every day at five in order to get two or three good hours of work in at his home office before coming to the university. Skinner himself projects an immediate kind of warmth and openness to visitors, as though he were truly anxious to learn about their work and to talk with them. He is a thin and somewhat worn-looking man whose wavy light brown hair, which is lightly touched with gray, has grown long and curly at the back of his head. "I am surprised people can find my office," he says in a low and steady voice. "I used to have my name out there but people keep stealing it, so I don't bother to put it up anymore."

He offers me a chair next to his desk and says that believing has always been a subject of great interest to him. He wears thick glasses, and his clothes have the rumpled look one might expect in a busy professor. He seems genuinely anxious to discuss the subject of faith and, during our conversation, makes occasional notes for himself on the subjects that have been covered. He makes the first of these after I describe some research in which creedal beliefs seem to be contrasted with experiential beliefs.

"Yes, yes," he says, "what we believe in through experience is shaped by contingency. Gradually these things get into creeds. The individual really does not have to analyze it himself. But somebody does analyze it and finally makes some judgments on what people seem to agree on about beliefs. They write it down to give people a short cut about how to live. That's how the rules or laws of the Church are developed. They tell us how to behave well so that we will not be punished; they show us how we can escape from the punitive contingencies of life." He turns back from the note he has just made and continues. "In other words, you can save yourself a lot of hard knocks in life if you can follow these rules. If you obey them, certain things will happen. Now that is all very different from any kind of mystical rapport that we might see as a different kind of experience of faith. The same thing is true of economics. You set up a contract through which you agree to work in view of certain outcomes. This is very different from working for yourself and getting the rewards of the experience of doing what you want to for yourself. That's more like experiential faith, I think. Perhaps we should contrast a mystical versus a legal faith. You get very far away from the mystical when you have to put things down in creeds or rules. Unfortunately, however, we need the rules in order to keep people from being hurt."

I ask him about his view of man. It has always seemed to me that he pictures man as very vulnerable and that part of his motivation in designing things like air cribs, educational teaching machines, or *Walden Two* itself, has been to protect people from some of the harsh and wounding things that occur regularly in life. Just as the air crib saves parents from the worry that a child will fall out the window or down the stairs, so the teaching machine saves the individual from the pain of bad instructors, and the Utopian village might create the environment in which people would do more right things than wrong things. Skinner seems to reveal, in his tones and his direction, a deep, almost tender, feeling for the human state. Is he preoccupied with the vulnerability of man? He nods his head as though this should be obvious to anyone who reads him carefully. "That is why we see the emergence of governments and religious institutions, and institutions of all sorts. These institutions and their rules and regulations have saved the individual from his own exploration of the world, from having to start at the beginning with everything. Institutions try to help us understand something about life so that we can make our way through it by building on the past. The question right now that concerns me, however, is the future. I am very concerned about that and about whether we are really free to have a future or not. I am concerned about the mechanisms that control the individual so that he will respond in terms of the best interests of society and, therefore, in his own best interest."

Skinner gestures toward Boston beyond his windows and says, "Now belief has something to do with the future; it is

related to the probability that something will happen. That
is one of the aspects of belief we all have to be concerned
with. In religion you traditionally speak of a long-distance
future. It is the same way with government. By setting up a
government you are saying that you believe in the future
and that you're going to try to affect that in the best possible
way. If we believe in man and the future, we have to concern ourselves with it right now. We're planning for that
future, by understanding the processes that will, in fact,
control man in this future. There will be nothing accidental
about these things. They are going to be there. We can either
take a hand in designing them intelligently now, or we will
find ourselves controlled by things we do not understand.

"This is always a difficult area for institutions, like government and the Churches, because they get concerned about
their own survival, about their own future. They put that
first. That is the way Machiavelli operated. The prince
maintains order for his own benefit, but in the long run, all
the people gain from that. Long-term consequences are by-
products of the immediate advantages of those who are
governing. That is why the Church has always used sanctions: in order to preserve its own control. But this kind of
thing produces long-range good effects through the stability
it achieves. Religion, in this sense, points to the future and,
of course, when it claims the power to mediate blessedness
or damnation it is taking a very long-range future into account.

"The people who run governments and Churches know
that they wouldn't survive unless they were selfish in the
present, that they would not attain these long-range advantages for the people if they didn't act that way. I think
our big problem right now, however, is finding people who
will take the future into account in their planning right now.
I am talking about things that require belief from us."

Skinner turns toward his desk and makes a brief notation
before turning back toward me and, frowning as though
dealing with an idea that is new to him, says, "Religion has

always reinforced the idea that we need some people who don't expect too much from the present. These are the kind of people we probably need in order to have some kind of a future. By that I mean people who are willing to take vows of poverty and celibacy. Perhaps they are essential because they focus us on our future and make us aware of our responsibility for it. In the nineteenth century we had that in the press. It came to be called the Fourth Estate because it had no power. It could afford to take a long look. It is supposed to be the same way for the good teacher in an academic setting who is somewhat free from present concerns. He can also take a long look at the future. Believing means that we all have to be able to do that. It is better to be able to do something about the future now than to wait and have the future do something about us.

"So if you make gluttony a sin, it restrains people in the present. It does something to us now that enables us to move toward the future more intelligently. The trouble is that institutions often get so tied up with the present that they find it hard to be benevolent. They get so tied up with surviving, with keeping themselves going, that they no longer do the right things that will help everybody in the long run. The more they must survive for themselves, the less they can do for us.

"I think that our most important problem in America is that people do not seem able to delay immediate gratifications in view of the future. We have to try to understand how we can learn to forego these in order to reach the future. I think this is all involved with a kind of believing. How, in other words, do we get people to take a cold shower now for the sake of the warm glow they get afterwards? This, I believe, is the big ethical question of the day: How do we make the right decisions in the present in order to be able to secure our future? The institutional Churches have always been a great help in this regard because they arrange additional reinforcers that make people look toward the future while making sacrifices in the present. Religion has always helped people to do that, to be heroic in the present in view of a better future. The only place we have ever seen that reversed is with the Kamikaze pilots in Japan. They gave them the rewards, the fullness of life, beforehand, a very unusual thing. The difficulty right now is that some people think that we can scare people into changing in the present in order to avoid a disastrous future. That kind of avoidance of punishment is never as effective as one that is based on rewards instead. The prophets of gloom do us a disservice; scaring people, in science or religion, has never really helped them much to prepare for doing the right things in the future."

I ask him how he understands the nature of faith. "The supernatural is the object of religious faith, although I have not focused on that. I have never been moved much by the idea that we should believe because it all seems impossible. We use the word *think* rather than *know* when our belief is weak. I think we make a distinction there as; if I couldn't see very well, I might say I *think* this is a phone, but when I get a better look at it I can say I *know* this is a phone. We use the word believe as against know. I believe in something. That's different from knowing it or just thinking about it. You could always go with Pascal's wager, the bet that we win whether God exists or not," and Skinner chuckles as he says it, "but I think that is immoral. I really don't think God welcomes that kind of bargain. But people believe in some explanatory system and they do it in terms of what has happened to them. What has happened to them is an effect of other people or institutions. They believe that unless they are inclined to behave in certain ways, they won't get through life. Man is born with a great predisposition to be changed, and this is conditioned by the people or institutions that surround him.

"If you mean a probability of behaving, belief is a concept that emphasizes the probability of response, some measure of the frequency with which we will do something. Perhaps that probability of response, that we will act or that things will happen in a certain way, is a main aspect of believing. I think that is close to the concept of believing."

I ask him why it seems so difficult for people to believe in what he has written or demonstrated in his scientific research, why it is that a man who has tried to design things to be helpful for men should bring down such a storm of criticism on his own person. In the reviews, I note, he, rather than his ideas, is criticized. "You'd think people would understand," he says shaking his head, "that we could avoid hurt to each other. You know they hanged me in effigy down in Indiana last week. But I'm not really saying anything new. All I'm saying is that we have to modify our immediate gratification if we are going to design environments that will be beneficial for us as a group. I think perhaps we have so pandered to immediate gratification that any suggestion that we give it up becomes very threatening to people. That may be why they react so strongly to me. I'm just amazed at these things. I was in New York the other day and, out of interest in finding out what it was all about, I went to this sexually explicit movie. There were a lot of young couples in there and it was the most offensive thing I have ever seen. It was the most utter degradation I have ever seen pictured on the screen. Now it's kind of a camp thing that these young couples seem to enjoy. It's things in this line that I am talking about. There is something very wrong with this just as there is with the drug culture. This emphasis on now and getting everything right now; there is so much emphasis on the 'right to enjoy' that thinking about the future and making sacrifices for it seems old fashioned. There is a fantastic concern with the present in this country; all I'm really trying to do is to say that we have to look beyond this if we're going to be truly human.

"Perhaps we should learn more about China; that is a country that I would really like to visit. The young Chinese live by a strict sexual and moral code; they eat simple food and wear this very simple padded clothing. A Westerner looks at a young Chinese and says, 'He's not free.' Ah"—

Skinner raises his eyebrows as a detective might who is suddenly going to point out the fact that everybody else missed—"but does he himself feel free? That is the question. Mao may have pulled this trick off by having given his people the right re-enforcement, by helping them to see that things are getting better every year. He may have let them see that the improvement of their country is contingent on their behavior. I think most of these people really do feel free and they feel proud and good about what they are achieving. Now how many Americans really feel free? Look at the students hanging around bored over at Harvard Square. Or how many people do you know who tell you they feel trapped in the middle of their lives? I think what we have to study is how various cultures make a future possible, and I believe we are in serious trouble in this country because we have neglected to do this."

What, I ask, is the role of religion in this? "Well, religion has traditionally pointed to this world as one of suffering and raised our eyes to another world where we would be freed from it. It is what Unamuno says, 'Sorrow binds us together.' Or it is like the labor leaders in the early days of the movement in this country. They had to increase the misery of their people in order to get them to work for greater achievements later on. There may be something in all that. People do have to learn to make sacrifices here and now. St. Benedict designed a world to enable you to be like Jesus. I have always been interested in monasteries. The rule said that if you enjoyed life, you wouldn't be like Jesus. If you want to be happy later, do what Jesus would do. I think that emphasis can be overdone so that people don't enjoy anything in life." Skinner laughs gently as he distracts himself for a moment, "I think the main problem with the Catholic Church right now is that it should move its headquarters to some other city. I think the Pope gets very bad advice in Rome . . .

"We keep emphasizing the way Jesus used miracles as a way of bettering people. Suppose he did it in some other way.

Perhaps it is unfortunate that we have a vision of Jesus as a miracle worker. We should remember that he was a slave and what he wanted to do, of course, was to relieve the internal rage of people who have to live in a slave state. That's the thing that's so terrible about it—the rage people experience when they are trapped in some state like that. What Jesus had to do was to salvage the dignity of men who were in a bad situation. I think that is exactly what he did with the Sermon on the Mount, one of the parts of Scripture I think about a great deal. What he said in effect was that the slave, by his behavior, could control his enemies, could take their power away. That was an extraordinary insight.

"One of the problems that Churches have is that in trying to keep the institutional aspect alive they may use power in a bad way. Then people walk away from the Churches—not from the idea of religion, but from their bad uses of power. People can do this for not irreligious reasons. That's the great strength of some religious faith. If a person commits himself to it, he removes himself from the power of those who try to control him. That's what happens when a person takes the vow of poverty; he or she is saying in effect that they're not going to be controlled by money.

"I have many Catholic friends. One of my closest is Sister Annette Walters who teaches psychology. She was a former student of mine. When she last came to visit me she was out of her religious habit, and I suddenly realized that she had a new kind of power, that the strength of her own personality and intelligence showed through because it was not obscured by that habit and by the need to relate to people in terms of the role it defined. This is the kind of thing that is going on in the Catholic Church; people are walking away from bad uses of power and discovering how strong they can be when they do it."

I ask him if many men and women of good will from different backgrounds do not seem to be converging in the same circle of values at the present time. "I think that's true.

You can even see it in things as far afield as Marxism. What people are realizing—and this is certainly at the heart of Christianity—is that you have to do the right thing by man. But you have to design this. I do see encouraging things happening. You know the human organism is a wonderful thing. It has great potential and everything depends on what you do for it after birth. Our greatest judgment may come to us because we do not make the most out of what a newborn child can be. That is a way of not accepting responsibility for the future. That is why ritual can be so helpful and important in religious institutions these days. It helps us understand the script of life; it helps us understand the mood of our own experience. I do think, however, that the Church should try to remove all the punitive techniques which it has used to try to make people behave better. That's as bad as physical punishment, the kind of thing you find in the Irish schools. That's one of the most awful traps you can get caught in. People will simply not improve just to avoid a terrible future. We ought to help people walk toward the future with a kind of a glow about it because they are not threatened when they know they are doing the right thing. I think something like Billy Graham's evangelism is very shoddy. Billy tells people that they are saved, that now they are out of trouble. Come and be saved, he tells them, but that is not helping them to prepare themselves for the future either."

What, I wonder, would he like his grandchildren to believe? Leaning back in his chair, Skinner becomes reflective. "I think both my daughters have turned out well. They are very nice and I am very fond of them. I was raised a Presbyterian and I gave it up in adolescence. I felt unhappy and guilty about it for years. Neither my wife nor I are religious. I look to this world for my reinforcers; I am concerned with this world and doing something about it. So we haven't had any regular religion and we never taught our children any religion. I remember once one of the neighbors spirited one of our daughters off to Mass because she thought she was being raised so poorly. Well, we never did give them anything in the way of supernatural reasons for life but I think both of my daughters are highly moral. Recently my younger daughter married a man who was also without religious faith. They designed their own wedding ceremony and I read one of Shakespeare's sonnets as part of it, you know the one that has the lines, 'Love is not love that alters when it alteration finds.' It was a beautiful ceremony. I think that these young couples really believe in something and that they are really trying to make sacrifices for each other, but it isn't anything in the way of traditional belief. I know my grandchildren are not going to be educated religiously." He pauses for a moment, but it is difficult to say what he is communicating in his silence. "I'm sorry my children did not get more contact with the Bible. I knew it and read it very thoroughly when I was a young man. You can discover amazing things in it and sometimes when I am in a hotel room I get out the Bible and spend a long time reading it. It has great messages in it . . .

"I think my daughters believe in something but it is certainly not a formalized religion, and I don't know whether this will do for people in general. It takes an awful lot of management to do away with miracles and sanctions for the ordinary person. Perhaps that is religion at an elementary level, and you can't easily do away with those things. Do you remember that scene in my novel *Walden Two*? It's the scene in which Frazier assumes the pose of being crucified. It was a scene that had to be in the book in order to make it ridiculous. Do you remember the question that it asked? What is love but positive reinforcement? Or the other question. What is positive reinforcement but love? . . ."

The clock has passed lunch time and Skinner, in a truly thoughtful voice, says, "Now you can't go without having something to eat." He orders some sandwiches and he continues to reflect on his life, on believers and others he has known. "Some of these unbelievers are pretty harsh and uncritical in their thinking. I was at a symposium the Jesuits

held in New York last year and some of the old die-hard critics of the Catholic Church were there. I got kind of tired of
their old statements after a while and decided to leave early,
but I went up to the Jesuit in charge and I said, "I think you
fellows won every round."

The sandwiches arrive and Skinner suggests that we eat
them with spoons because the tuna fish salad has a way of
spilling out if you try to eat it by more ordinary means. There
is a tenderness and a sadness about this man that has seldom
been communicated in anything I have read about him. I
decide to tell him my impression, that I believe that his
tenderness is a strong part of his efforts to design a world
whose environment would be more congenial and less hurting for human beings. He nods at what I say and turns
thoughtful for a long time. He is obviously hurt by his
critics. "Some of them are uncivil in the way they address
themselves to me," he says, in a voice that is part surprise
and part melancholy. "I've been picketed a lot recently and
they give out these handbills that have superimposed my
head on that of a rat. I'm even blamed for *A Clockwork
Orange* and aversive therapy. When I was in England recently there was a whole issue of a magazine accusing me of
being responsible for aversive therapy." He shakes his head
and takes a sip of his tea as he recalls it, "Now, anybody
should know that I have never had anything to do with
aversive therapy, that I do not believe in punishment as
effective in changing human behavior. I thought *A Clockwork Orange* was a terrible motion picture, very hurting,
even in the way it was photographed . . ."

He asks me what I think about the Catholic Church at the
present time, and I tell him that I hope it can be a home for
all men, something in the way Robert Frost speaks of home
as "the place where, when you have to go there, they have to
let you in." He smiles and says, "You know I quoted those
lines just the other day at a meeting. They were discussing
whether a former colleague of ours could return to teach
here or not. Robert Frost was a great influence on me at

one time. He encouraged me as a writer." Skinner gets up
and crosses to a filing cabinet, saying, "I have a letter from
Frost here written to me many years ago. I have to think
of how to preserve it, I guess, but, here, have a look at it."
He shows me a letter of comment on some short stories
written by Skinner almost forty years ago. It is a warm
letter in which Frost tells the young Skinner that his stories
are as good as anything he has seen, and that they are told
straight and true. It is clear that Skinner is still proud of
that letter and, as we sit down again, he talks once more of
himself as a writer. He is talking as the tender man now,
the man who cannot fathom why he is so misunderstood.
"The trouble with me at that time was I didn't have anything to say. But I have always worked at my writing. I
have always wanted it to be clear and without any tricks. I
spoke to six thousand people at a university last week. I
didn't tell any jokes. I didn't entertain them. I didn't con-
descend to them. I respected them. I said what I did as
clearly as I could. They were all quiet and seemed to
respond." He is saying something about what he truly believes in and it revolves around respecting man and doing
your best, in whatever role you have in life, to make the way
easier for him. "Yes, I think that is what we must do, the
very best we can, as honestly as we can, for all mankind . . ."

The plane to Albuquerque rocks through a late-winter snowstorm growling its way across the moonlike surface of the Southwest. At the airport, James Shannon, now wearing a corduroy driving jacket and sporting longer hair and a tobacco-colored mustache, is the same gentle man he was when he wore the gold-chained black clerical garb of a Roman Catholic bishop. As the possessor of a doctorate in American studies from Yale University, he knows better than most the significance of a Catholic bishop's leaving his official position and marrying, both of which he did in the same summer that men landed on the moon and Teddy Kennedy drove off a bridge at Chappaquiddick. Since then he has been attending law school at the University of New Mexico, preparing for a new career which he does not perceive as entirely discontinuous with his former one. His face lights up as he sees me, and I am warmed by the sight of a man I have always respected deeply. In the times I have seen him since his marriage he has always struck me as still a mediator, a natural kind of priest who always seeks understanding between people even at cocktail parties, a man whose loyalty to the Roman Catholic Church is unchanged despite the dramatic transformation in his own life.

The sky is clearing over the airport as we head down the road in his veteran Volkswagen. We head across the valley toward the Sandia Mountains which are hidden by the cloud of snow that still hangs in front of them and half way across Albuquerque. He tells of his eagerness for me to visit with him and his wife, Ruth, once secretary to former Senator Kenneth Keating of New York, and now a personnel director at a large local company. Jim Shannon describes his law school career. Speaking softly, he tells how much his wife Ruth meant as he struggled with the decision of whether to take on this additional schooling or not. "I had been in school for so many years," he says, laughing, "that it seemed a hard thing to start all over again. I did get some pretty good offers to become a college president again. There was one that was hard to turn down because it offered a Lincoln Continental along with everything else. But," and Jim grows silent for just a moment, "I really felt that with the law I could do something for the suffering and the poor, something for justice that would fit in with what I have always believed in." He tells of the fact that he will graduate in a few months and that he has accepted a job with a large law firm in the city. "I told them there were lots of good reasons not to take me on. I really put it to them, but they said they wanted me anyway. They are a sensitive and liberal group and they understand that I want to give some of my time to the kind of causes and people who ordinarily can't get legal representation. I'm looking forward to working with them . . ."

We pull into a muddy side yard by a veterinary where Jim must pick up some pills for the new puppy that is ailing at home. "I have found that little things like this are a big part of life for most people," he says with his broad Irish grin, "that life is made up of a lot of little things like this." In a few moments we are driving into the yard of the low adobe house, set on a couple of acres of land, where the Shannons live. "It was a stop on the old trail, and they kept the horses in one room and the men were able to sleep in the other. We were lucky to be able to find such a place." It is obvious that he takes great pride in his own home and that he is happy to be able to open it in hospitality to a friend. The snow has turned to sleet and it is pleasant to be inside by his fireplace and to enjoy a drink together while Ruth prepares supper. Jim is very

solicitous about Ruth and moves out to assist her with some
of the preparations, a characteristic move that will recur
often during the evening. It was Ruth, Jim had told me in
the car, who had given an unquestioning *yes* when he first
brought up the idea of law school; Ruth has provided him
with a source of support and strength during the long
months and years of preparation for a legal career in the
middle of life. There are mementos of Jim's life as a priest
and bishop throughout the house, his Episcopal Coat of
Arms and the decree of the pope naming him a bishop.
There are pictures and souvenirs of the places and people
who were so much a part of his life in Minneapolis where
he served as an auxiliary bishop after having been president
of St. Thomas College. "Believing is an interesting subject,"
he begins, poking at the fire again, "and I have thought
about it a lot. What a man believes in is really important.
I think there is some big movement going on in the world
right now, some new sense of man's developing unity. It
really is a global village now, and I think our faith is very
much related to a new understanding that we all belong to
the same family. The idea of the unity of the race and of
some first force setting it in motion: Many other things
fall into place if you can begin with this. It is a very central
notion. Barbara Ward talks about it quite a bit, about our
need to come at last to the idea of unity, that we are all
related somehow in God's creation. It's one thing to come
to do this as a scientist, but I think it's quite another thing
to come to it out of a sense of personal relationships and our
common humanity. I think that idea is very important for
everybody to think about. It certainly has been an important one in my life."

Jim goes out to look at the ailing puppy for a moment and
I cannot help think how far his journey has taken from
those days when he was popularly considered one of the
American Catholic Church's best and brightest, a leader who
would sooner or later take on major leadership responsibilities. And of how, after a painful few years of conflict

with the Church's official position on birth control and a
period of intense criticism and censure on the part of other
bishops, he came to step away from it all, from red hats
and influence, away from security and into a new and uncharted darkness. "I was once on the committee of the bishops on relations with unbelievers," Jim says as he returns,
"but I am not sure there is such a creature as an unbeliever.
Men always have to believe in something. They couldn't
get along without it. I think it's just too easy to talk about
people without faith or without belief. That's just too simple.
All men are seeking for some vision of the universe they
live in, and good men coming from different directions finally climb to the same plateau where they are no longer
concerned about the vocabulary each one of them uses. They
recognize in and with each other that they are talking about
the same thing. I think something like that is happening to
help people of sensitivity and good will to get back to this
unity we all share. You know some people have called me a
faithless servant," and there is a look of pain in his eyes
as he recounts some of the other things that critics have
said about him since he withdrew from his bishop's role,
"but I still believe and I think what I am trying to do is a
continuation of the ministry I gave my life to before." The
conversation cannot help but go back to the life he led as
a priest and bishop and to that source of conflict about
birth control which led him to question the official
Church's stand. He seems to be feeling it all again as he
speaks.

"When I was pastor in those last few years I would try
to avoid the confessional box on Saturdays. I would tell my
associates there early in the week that I would be away at
that time. The reason is that I knew that any counsel I
gave on birth control would surface at bridge parties all
over the parish. I was really concerned about the position
of the official ecclesiastical organization; I understood that
they had to have rules even though they did not seem to fit
the pastoral situation as I saw it. I never said, 'The pope is

wrong.' I think it's better to let the Church say that Jim Shannon can't function the way it expects he should. I think the categories that are so easy to us about saying who is right or wrong slip away then. What do you say about this anyway? Who is right and who is wrong? What are we to tell people about life? That they are always to choose loneliness and separation? I have known a lot about loneliness and separation myself, and I don't want to be a hero for those who have bad motives and just want to criticize the Church." Jim sips his drink and looks thoughtful for a moment; all one can hear is the crackling of the fire and the peppering of sleet against the windows, "You know the Church is my home. It is the only spiritual home I will ever have, and right now I am not welcome in it. Ruth and I go to Mass at the Newman Center at the university. Ruth is perfectly free to marry; the ecclesiastical impediments are all on my side. I'm the obstacle. We are frequently spotted by the celebrant and he asks us to bring up the gifts at the offertory. It is very hard not to be able to receive the Sacrament of the Eucharist." He says this in a soft and sad voice, in a tone that grieves for the pain he causes for his wife as much as for the pain he knows himself. Yet it is not a voice lacking hope; is there an intimation, a hunch that some day he might yet be able to receive the Eucharist again?

He shakes himself a little, as though to shed the uncomfortable thoughts, and looks toward me. "I have an abiding conviction of the eventual triumph of good, not so much good over evil as good over bad intentions. I think we make progress by millimeters, that's the only way you can measure it and I hope my new life contributes to that. I don't expect to be a legal hero of the Southwest, but there are a lot of hard questions about situations out here—very practical ones that demand that you believe in something in order to respond to them. What do you do to help the poor who have eviction notices in their hands? I have learned some new tools and have mastered some new instruments that are going to enable me to give some answers to that. I think we have to tap the private sector in order to respond to these difficulties. I want to work for these people in the valley and I know I will have time for it with this law firm." He stands up as Ruth comes into the room with cheese and crackers. Jim holds her arm gently and turns to me, saying, "We have to believe in what we are doing and have some inner personal conviction that we are doing the best we can with the life that we have. You come to a certain point where you have to trust God. That's what Ruth and I do. We pray and we trust. Don't think I haven't awakened a hundred times at three o'clock in the morning and asked myself what I was doing and how I got into all this. But I believe I'm trying to do the right thing."

You sense how Jim perceives that his life is all of one piece, symbolized perhaps by his wearing of his bishop's ring on one hand and his wedding ring on the other. He is not a changed man; he has moved in a new direction with an old center of gravity. It is clear that he would like to speak about the days in which he struggled with his decision to leave; Jim speaks without bitterness, as a man who feels that his faith is unchanged, as a man who feels that although his conscience led him out of his role in the Church it has not led him out of the Church altogether. At dinner he begins to talk again about his life as a pastor back in Minneapolis.

"We had a funeral the first day I was in that parish. He was a distinguished professional man. The widow and the husband had been fairly close to another couple and the husband was distinguished in the same field. Well, sometime after the funeral this widow took a trip to California where she met this former associate of her husband's and discovered that his wife had become an alcoholic and divorced him, leaving him on his own. He began to drink himself. When the widow went to see him he was really glad that she had come. He said to her, 'I'm losing my grip and I need help. Will you help me?' There she was sitting in the parlor telling me this story and asking me about it. Could she in good conscience go and marry this man who had been divorced? She had consulted with her children who had all gone to Catholic colleges. They decided, after thinking it over, that she should go marry him and take care of him. Looking back on that meeting I realize how important that experience was for me. I really had to face something about the way I was dealing with people. Here was this lovely gracious woman who didn't want any canonical discussion from me. All she wanted to know was whether I would say *yes* or *no*. I was playing a cozy game with this lovely lady, and I realized I was being false and not treating her with dignity although I was trying to treat her with some kind of ecclesiastical rectitude. So I said to her, 'You owe it to God and yourself and your children to go to take care of that man.' I knew I was right and I knew I was wrong." Jim stands up to add some wood to the fire and turns back to me again. "I was aware at the time of the discussions that were going on about allowing marriages like this in certain situations. Monsignor Stephen Kelleher of the New York chancery had done some work about it. I also knew that I had been avoiding the confessional to avoid facing these critical questions, that I was doing a lot of double talk, nothing but double talk. I just couldn't keep doing that.

"What I truly believe in is the integrity and the rectitude of good people. I think that is where you hear the meaning of belief. That's the meaning of the old Latin phrase, *Sensus fidelium*, the sense of the faithful. That is the very thing, the common judgment of good people, that has repudiated the pope's encyclical on birth control. We had to get back to that level of human experience. That's what you see in the work of any good priest. Take somebody like Monsignor Robert Fox who works with the Spanish in New York. You can believe in the authenticity of his experience with his people. That's why people recognize what they believe in when they have been through the same kind of experience

together. I remember being at a meeting of the Young Presi-
in, "For some reason I don't understand, God has showered
stood up to state their grievances at the institutional Church.
Their candor was quite touching. A Jewish gentleman in
the group said something like this. 'My wife and I have
bled to death over this war in Vietnam. We can't buy the
canned messages the Church gives out, but where do we
go and where can we fit? We envy you with your antecedent
assurance on truth. We don't find sacrifice difficult.
It's something we want to believe in.' They were a remarkable group, each one of them looking for the institutional Churches to do better in speaking to their own
human experience. I couldn't help feeling that, as they spoke
from their various backgrounds, they were organizing some
new kind of institutional Church, some new kind of presence of understanding that takes the best out of all the
traditions. These people are all meeting in some new place
where they recognize how much they believe in together . . ."

"The problem with many of the institutional Churches
is that they haven't maintained their authority of service.
They are not really in touch with what people are yearning
about; they insist on an authority that comes from outside
of experience. People just don't go for that. They will respond to authorities when they seem endorsable, when they
seem in touch with them. I heard someone say to a Santa
Fe politician recently, 'We would gladly lose with you.'
That's when people believe in somebody, and that's the
way the Churches have to approach this human family
that's getting a better sense of its own unity."

The evening draws on and Jim and his wife drive me
back to my motel. They stop to join me in a last drink together. The lounge is filled with colorfully dressed people
who have come for the balloon races that had been post-
poned because of the bad weather. Through the smoky
haze, the room shudders under the impact of rock music.
Jim is thinking back on the events that led up to his de-

parture, about the moment at the administrative board meeting of the bishops when the Cardinal Archbishop of Los Angeles asked that the other bishops censure him because of his participation in a nationwide television show. It hurt him then and it hurts him still. He describes how his own archbishops had failed to defend him, how one had absented himself from the meeting at which the vote was taken and how the other had abstained. "The bishops voted two to one against me, to censure me for accepting the job of speaking for them which I had been asked to fill by the bishop in charge of communications. I was supposed to fly home with my archbishop that night, but I decided against it. I rented a car and drove to Annapolis, Maryland, to St. John's College where I knew the president. He said that if I wanted some time to think things out, I would be welcome to spend some time at their college there or at the one they had in Santa Fe. That was really the trigger, the catalyst that started me thinking about where I really stood and whether I could continue in my role of trying to speak out for what I believed was the real experience of people in a Church that was ruling over them from a distance. My superiors were good men, I know that. But they were thoroughly conditioned to do exactly what the Church expected of them." He shakes his head, knowing that he has been criticized for making the move that has brought him so far from the Roman-collared world he knew so well. He has mixed feelings, but he still does not feel he was wrong to challenge the lies and distortions that he felt he met in his last months as an active bishop. He tells of how the Apostolic Delegate flatly denied saying something to him which, in fact, he had said to Jim not once but twice. "So I said to him, 'With all due respect, you're lying.' My archbishop said, 'Now, Jim, the Apostolic Delegate is an honorable man.' I looked at my archbishop and said, 'I am an honorable man . . .'" There is no doubt that this tragic episode, in the course of which Bishop Shannon was invited into exile into another country because of his questions about the birth control teaching of the Church, was extremely hard on him and that the wound is still not completely healed.

There are those who say Jim Shannon was hurt too easily by the criticism he received from other bishops, that he should have been tougher and stayed on, that his leaving has hurt the faith of many other persons. Is it faith that dictates this hindsight scenario or some kind of worldly wisdom about how to stay happy and successful in the organization? What would have been the price for him—and for all of us—if he had remained a bishop and had not spoken out on the issues of conscience? How has belief best been served? It is not an easy question to answer.

It is clear that Jim Shannon needs someone to believe in him, some response from out of the darkness that recognizes and affirms him as much as Ruth does. The night draws on and both the balloonists and the rock music get louder; they cannot drown out or hide the hurt that this believing man still carries within him. One senses that visits from old friends are important, that they are like voices saying *yes,* we understand and we believe in you, and we know that the Church is broader and deeper and richer than some of its officials think.

In a few minutes he and Ruth must leave because they have a long day ahead of them. It is snowing quite heavily and because of the arrangement of the parking lot Jim must back down an incline and into the darkness, his flashing headlights a last goodbye in the bitter cold. In a minute the car is turned around and he is heading back into the cloud that still lies across the city.

He has journeyed a long way into darkness, I think, but he has left neither his faith nor his love for the Church behind. It is a strange and troubling story, a scenario not yet fully worked out. It is easy to write that he should never have left the Church, that at all costs he should have remained within it to become a great leader in a long and honor-filled career. It is easy to write that he has made a mistake, especially if we judge by the traditional notion that only those who remain within the official Church can speak to us of the meaning of faith. We have not yet heard the ending of Jim Shannon's story. It may turn out quite differently than anyone can now suppose. It is hard to know about Jim Shannon's future, but it is very clear that he has one.

A MAN AND A WOMAN

The moon is rising above Camelback Mountain and the city of Scottsdale, twinkling in the clear air, is spread out below the home of Don and Ruth, as down-to-earth and loving a couple as any I have ever met. Married twenty-six years and the parents of four sons, they are intensely interested in religion and have agreed to talk to me about the subject of believing. Don, a strongly built and highly successful man with the kind of personality that lights up any room he enters, begins in tones that are a mixture of reflection and enthusiasm. Ruth, a small and pretty blonde, looks at him with the kind of patient glance that projects listening and involvement. They are not religious fanatics—and that is one of the reasons I have asked to interview them—but they are believers; and it is clear just in looking at them that they very much believe in each other.

"I believe in God and myself," Don begins, "in Jesus really, more than in God the Father. I'm a convert and I have always been interested in religion. During World War II I had three roommates, one was a Catholic, one was a Jew, and one was a Mohammedan. We were always on report for sitting up arguing about religion. But that was the first time I realized that there was a broader total field that you have to look at, that these were people who were looking at the world through different eyes but saying the same thing." Don touches Ruth's arm and goes on. "I became a Catholic for our marriage." Ruth smiles and says, "I remember our first date. We had a great time and at the end of the evening you said to me, 'I bet you're a Catholic.' When I asked you why, you said that every girl you ever liked was a Catholic, so you weren't very far out of the Church."

Don smiles and says, "Certain things flash through my mind. My own spiritual growth; I remember visiting Montreal almost twenty-three years ago at that shrine of Brother André's. I felt a very spiritual experience at that time. It helped me to sense my relationship with my God. We can talk to each other. That gave me a sense of that special relationship. God was very personal as far as I was concerned. He knew me. He was not untouchable. Once you realize that, you can develop faith in yourself. Believing in yourself is very important. If you can't stand what you look at when you shave every morning, you're going to have a bad day. You have to come to terms with believing in who you are.

"My next big impression was from a Jesuit priest, an elderly man who spent a year at the retreat house we went to. He sputtered all the time he was there because he had been forced to go there. He had a wonderful basic pure belief, however, and he did a lot of wonderful things, like helping to bring women into the retreat house for the first time. He had a wonderful outlook and helped people to believe in Jesus. He didn't believe that people with free will could ever turn their backs on God, and he also believed that God had to be absolute in his charity toward us. He had the post-Vatican II feeling long before."

Ruth joins in, her eyes lighting up in recollection of this priest friend of theirs, "That was in the days when people never talked about love. He helped us to do that, to see how much that was a part of our faith." Don adds, "Yes, that reinforces your belief. I can speak to my God directly. I believe in prayer. God is not cruel or vindictive. No matter what I have done I can discuss it with him. I have a feeling," and he pauses for a thoughtful moment, "that God expects something of me. I may never know quite what, but I know I have to try to do what he wants me to do. Maybe in my work. I just don't know. It may have something to

do with my family or my wife or my children. Whatever it
is, I have to keep trying to figure out what God wants. As
long as I've got faith in myself I can wrestle this problem
through."

I look at Don and Ruth and realize that although they
are speaking separately, they are very much one in their
nods and occasional unselfconscious squeezes of each
other's arms. "Anytime I've led from fear in my life, things
have collapsed. Anytime I begin from faith, that's when
everything falls into place. I have been very lucky and very
fortunate in my friends and family and in my very good
health. One of the things I have been most fortunate about
is living near the Franciscan Renewal Center down in
Scottsdale." Don points toward the twinkling valley below
as he describes what I myself have known as a quite remarkable gathering of priests, religious, and laity, a model in
many ways of what a living Church can be like in its response to people's spiritual needs. "These things have just
come into my life, however, and this kind of builds a selfish
feeling. I know God has done this and he expects me slowly
to figure out what he wants." Ruth, lighting a cigarette, joins
in, "For some reason I don't understand, God has showered
me with so much and protected me all my life long. People
have just come into my life to help me or to spare me from
difficult things. I remember when we moved to Dallas; we
were just there and I was pregnant and sitting at a shopping
center in the car when a woman came over and asked if she
could be of any help. She told me her husband was a doctor.
That night I had a problem and we called him. I lost the
child, but it was still a remarkable thing. I can't help but
think these people were sent to me. The only way I can reply
is to try to bring some joy into other people's lives, even a
smile to a stranger, or a word to an old person.

"That's why we like to have young people here all the
time and they seem to come. We're glad to have them. I just
hope they get something from our relationship. I just do my
little bit on a people-to-people basis. I hope somehow I can

help them have faith, the kind of faith I have been blessed
with, without preaching to them. I hope they can get it by
osmosis. I would never preach, but I do enjoy trying to share
things with others. It's very rewarding to give yourself to
others.

"And Don and I believe in each other. This is difficult to
verbalize, but I know that Don is one hundred per cent on
my side even though we have our differences. In the final
analysis, he is there. It's healthy to disagree, but we don't
disagree on goals. And I am part of his life and feel that.
That's necessary for me to help him in his business, with, for
example, the people he brings into town or brings out here.
I want to give them some warmth instead of just the usual
steak and a baked potato. I feel I do help him, that that's
part of the way we keep faith with each other."

Ruth smiles warmly as though seeing in her mind their
four strong sons, "Our children are very precious to us. We
are very family oriented and we enjoy having good times together. We had a captain, a young man of thirty, on a boat
we hired last year, and he just couldn't get over the fact that
a family could enjoy themselves so much together. That's
where it all is. Our boys all keep in touch with us; they have
strong ties and they bring their girls home. That means a
lot."

I ask Ruth about fidelity and what that means to them
while Don answers a phone call. "The greatest reason I can
give for our fidelity is that we both want it that way. Being
true, that's what we want out of life.

"Faith fills every moment of every day. Faith is very central in our lives. It's all part of the way we feel toward each
other. Faith is a big element in that, a part of the feeling of
warmth and openness that we try to give to each other. You
don't have to be a perfect specimen around here. You are
loved the way you are. We've given our children a lot of
freedom, but we really have never had any moment of concern. We've just had so much love in our family. I think
that's what has made the big difference; the most important

thing to us is our religion. That has helped to make our family one unit."

I ask Ruth about the greatest quality she sees in her husband. Without hesitation she answers. "Believability. I really believe in him as a person. I believe strongly that he's always on my side. It takes believing in each other to make a marriage work. Lots of people just don't have that. We have lots of love and I have always felt it very deeply. We think we have to give away what we've got. Don is very difficult sometimes; he's short tempered and he's a real softy with money. I once told him that he ought to put on a Santa Claus suit . . ."

What, I ask, is the role of the Church as an institution in their lives. Ruth answers, "I think the Church is very important. It stands there as someone to say you're doing okay. When I get hell and damnation, that turns me off. I think that's why the Church has failed young people. It hasn't adjusted to their way of thinking. I'm afraid our bishops are just in another world. They don't understand that they have to fulfill the needs of people. That's why the Franciscan Center has been so important to us. It draws people to it."

Don returns as she is talking about the Church and joins in immediately. "The Church has to be oriented to a new generation. The reason the Franciscan Center is so successful is that it radiates what the Church ought to be all about. It radiates love and happiness, almost like a mystery. Those people down there have a total love and respect for humanity. That place just radiates happiness in a way that you don't see in many other places. That's why the kids respond to them. Young people are looking for this kind of thing in many ways. That's why they go to join communes.

"There is a total feeling of liturgy down there, something that integrates your beliefs and your life. I never understood the meaning of liturgy until I could see its significance down there. God didn't mean religious practices to be drab and boring, but most of them are. God is a God of Love, a living God and you should enjoy worshiping Him. I'm afraid that many of our bishops are afraid of that. They don't realize the very thing they're preaching. God became a man to teach us what the right responses are, the ones we should have as human beings. Young adults have a very pure and uncontaminated belief, but they are hung up on organized religion as hypocritical. They just don't want to be part of something that's dishonest. I think the Catholic Church has fallen down on trying to be honest. Many Churches are structured for older people, and as institutions they are just going to have to die out. Part of the problem is, of course, that many parents don't care either. I think we have to get rid of these old things, the way Christ threw the merchants out of the temple. In other words, he threw out the old religions to replace them by asking us to be loving and to be honest with each other."

Ruth and Don, in speaking about youth, clearly have deep feelings. It is also obvious that the local Renewal Center has responded to their religious needs in a quite positive and helpful way. It is one of the few times that I have heard people speak of the liturgy as serving an integrating function between their beliefs and their lives. Don continues enthusiastically, "On Holy Thursday down at the Center they had a wonderful thing. They invited all the Rabbis from Phoenix to a Passover Dinner out in the courtyard. Then they passed from that into the Paschal meal, to the Liturgy of Holy Thursday. You could feel the whole sweep of our religious history in this experience. I told the bishop about it and the only question he could ask was, 'Did a full sixty minutes elapse between the meal and the Mass?' I think Jesus would say to him, 'Don't you understand what this is all about?'"

Ruth breaks in to tell her feeling about the Center. "Going over there has given me a new perspective on religion. It has let me be free. You know you have to be free in order to love. If you're in bondage, you can't love. You lose everything when you are forced to do it. But worshiping there and knowing the people there, I feel this freedom to love

God and to love my fellow man." Don adds, in a practical but concerned tone, "That's the only way you can root out your bigotry, all those feelings that destroy us. It's only in that kind of atmosphere that we can do something about the hang-ups that plague our country."

I ask him what they would like their sons and grandchildren to believe in and Ruth says, "I'd like them to believe in the dignity of the human person," and Don finishes the sentence, "and in Jesus and in themselves. I hope that each of my sons can have his own deep relationship with his loving God and willingly search out what he wants him to do in life. I pray that they will not lead from fear and that they will aim at the goals that are right for them. I want them to be honest with themselves." Ruth adds, "I want them to have freedom. It's very new for us and very precious, but I want them to have freedom to love God and their neighbor."

Don looks at Ruth with a kind of telling glance that speaks of a quarter of a century together and says gently, "Ruth's greatest quality is kindness, that very loving patience that she has shown to me all through our life together. You know, believing in each other has meant everything to us, but people should realize that a relationship of love changes. It was different twenty years ago and it's going to be different ten years from now. That's particularly true as you raise children. We were three and a half years before we had a child and that can lead you to being rather selfish. You have to have children in order to open yourself up, to make you tolerant, to help you sense the purpose of your life. Our faith has helped us to see the meaning of our family and our work, that all these things fit together."

Ruth says, "God has smiled on us," and Don adds, "I think God has a due bill out on us," to which Ruth quickly rejoins, "I don't believe that at all," and they both laugh gently together.

Don continues, looking back on the years they have spent together, "We've had a lot of rough times but you forget those. Life is a kind of roller coaster. I remember once I came home and all that was left of my pay check was $2.56. I've had a lot of other business dips. I've lost everything and have had to start over, but we've had faith in ourselves and Ruth has always had total faith in me. If your wife doesn't believe in you, you just cannot make it. I remember when I asked her to come out here. She came along really because she believed in me, and she's always known what was the right thing for me to do . . ."

Don and Ruth seem very unselfconscious in the way they speak about their believing and their voices are almost intermingled as they conclude. "Except for total belief I don't see how anybody can lead their lives or get any meaning out of it. You just have to turn to God. Do the best you can and leave it up to him. But never be afraid. If you believe enough in each other and God, you'll make it through anything."

JAMES EDWARD WALSH

Thirty miles north of New York City Bishop James Edward Walsh lives in retirement at Maryknoll. He was freed from a Chinese prison in 1970 after completing twelve years of a twenty-year sentence. He looks back from this hill that overlooks the Hudson Valley and almost sixty years as a priest, much of it in or connected with missionary activity in China. He is frail and worn looking, but his eyes are clear and his voice rises and falls in the soft and almost southern cadences of his western Maryland origins. Dressed in a clerical shirt and a comfortable old sweater, he is sitting in the corner of his study. He has been shy of interviews since his return from China and has tried to avoid public appearances or making any statements that might in any way be critical of the Chinese people. His has, however, been a life of duty, and I have the feeling that he considers seeing me something of a duty as well. The sunlight falls on his large full brow and lights up the powdery strands of hair that remain there. His hands and face have the brown spots of old age but he projects a core of strength beneath an outer frailness. He is a person who has been tempered by years of imprisonment and whose features, like some fine porcelain whose secrets disappeared with its maker, seem to have been strengthened and enriched by the passing years.

"Faith?" the Bishop speaks slowly but without hesitation, "All I know is in the catechism, 'the *substantia rerum non apparentium.*' We understand faith from God and his divine revelation through which we get some glimpse of his attributes." It is an answer out of a book he mastered a long time ago, one that he has accepted and lived by without swerving. It has served him well and there is a look of mild surprise on his face, the way a man might look when he is not sure if you are a doubting Thomas or not.

"If that isn't true . . ." but he does not finish his sentence. His voice becomes firmer as he goes on. "Many consider it subjective nonsense, but divine revelation is a great reality. There is a supernatural source for faith, although there are many natural reasons to support it as well. Faith is a grace by which we believe what God reveals to us." You almost feel that he has never seriously questioned or been troubled about the meaning of faith, that he has just simply believed as wholeheartedly as possible and that, when the test of his faith and character came, he was well prepared for it. He has emerged from the fires of trial with the initial faith of his life made deeper by them. It is not something to be picked apart or questioned. He strikes me as a good man who has somehow escaped the corruption of life which touches most of the rest of us.

"What is the most important part of faith?" the Bishop responds, repeating my question and thinking about it for a few moments. He speaks with strong conviction. "The central fact is that our Lord is the Son of God and that he came down to become a man and to redeem us on the cross. The incarnation is the most important part of our faith. That is at the heart of it all." He answers the questions without defensiveness but with a certain finality, as though little could be added if you really could grasp the significance of faith itself. I ask him what the hallmarks of a believer are, and smiling gently, he answers, "I don't know what points you could single out, but I think charity is the chief manifestation of it. The whole story of religion is one of charity. God is supreme charity. Then we have all the examples that Christ gave us." He pauses for a few moments and, moving away from what seems to me remembered statements, he becomes more personal, "I think that the great sign of faith is found in the lives of people who are able to love. The Chinese are naturally a very kind and sociable people. They are good to their neighbors and to their families. They are naturally that way, but I don't think they go as far as they can when they are inspired by faith. As pagans they have a surprising amount of charity. All of us who worked in China recognized that, but we felt that the Christian faith added a great deal. You know," and he looks more directly at me, "the Chinese have their faults too. Our Catholic people, however, had a higher standard than those among whom they lived. They were noted for their better conduct and that there was less immorality among them. You know the Chinese are very loose sometimes regarding the Sixth Commandment, and they could use vile language." There is something so simple about the way he recollects these people, something so innocent that I have a sense of a man who is more like an angel than anybody I have ever met. He laughs in an engaging way as he recalls the vile language, "I still have a lot of their sayings ringing in my ears but, you know, Christianity improved their family life and their observation of the Ten Commandments. Then religious vocations appeared and the Chinese responded quickly and well to the needs of the Church, and they really developed a great love for it." The Bishop rubs his hands together as a man might in front of a fire; perhaps he is warmed by his own recollections of a missionary world where the faith was brought as an unquestioned gift to people who then molded their Christianity on the Western model brought by most of the priests, ministers, and other religious personnel. It is still largely unquestioned in his view of things even though, in most missionary societies, the theology and psychology of missionary work is a subject of much soul searching. I ask him whether he can tell me something about the way he observed faith in the lives of people with whom he has worked.

"It is hard to know the history of any individual soul, and you know I wasn't a parish priest for many years so I didn't have much contact with individuals in the pastoral sense. I was a superior in China and then I was made a bishop, and that just makes you into a chief cook and bottle washer. I have had the misfortune of being in some kind of superior's job or administrative job almost all of my life in the priesthood. Still," and he laughs warmly, "I made many good friends among the Chinese people. I was really tied up, however, as a clerical administrator. I was trying to solve other people's problems, like the problems of priests. Father Thomas Quirk in Manchuria used to say that the hardest problem for a priest was to live without an assistant priest, and that the second hardest problem was for the priest to live with an assistant. There is really some truth in that. Those seem to be the sort of problems I dealt with all the time. I wish I had done more pastoral work."

I ask him about the amount of writing he had done all through his life, much of which has been published and has been well regarded critically. He had always struck me as something of a poet, a man who could see into persons and events without imposing the ecclesiastical or clerical apparatus on them. He is, however, surprising me by his answers; they seem to be coming from a man who long ago and for good gave himself over to living by the book. Obedience without questioning has been an important part of his life. He is a living example of the kind of achievement and adjustment that many fine men made in an age in which the faith was hardly questioned at all. His writing, it had always seemed to me, must have been spontaneous, something that allowed his real feelings to be expressed. But I am wrong here too; obedience dictated his writing as well. "Our first Superior General told me that I should write, so I applied myself to it over the years. I kept that up almost to the time I was finally imprisoned. You know, if you do a lot of writing, you have to write something good once in a while." He is at the edge of denying his own literary gifts, or feels that they flowered only in the context of obedient faith. One would put it too cruelly to say that his life had been absorbed by the system; that would not be correct and yet there is no doubt that the Church surrounded, supported, and validated the expression of his faith and his work. Despite all that and whether he himself recognized it, he never lost his spontaneity. It shows through as he goes on, "We had a really delightful little mission place in Shanghai. The Chinese people were constantly coming and going. There was a playground in the front that the children used to use all the time. I loved them very much and I got to know them. I tried to incorporate human interest about these people in all the things I wrote. You learn a lot from people. People in Shanghai were very sociable, very good and kind people, both the Catholics and the Protestants. They all had very strong reactions in their faith and belief, especially when the Communists came and tried to destroy their beliefs. I saw them hauled off day after day and many of them were imprisoned, although some would be released . . ." His voice has a sound of pride in it now and he nods his head in recollection of the believing Christian Chinese who are the proof, as he sees it, of everything he has given his life for.

"I remember an old man there who stood up and addressed the other Christians. He said, 'Now is the time for us to make up our minds. We're either Catholics or not. If we are, then we must listen to the Church and live by that.' He was one of those who later went to prison . . ."

The subject shifts to the changes in the Church. He has, after all, emerged as Rip Van Winkle might have, to find the Catholic Church transformed in many of its accidentals. He speaks gently in answer to my question. "I can't form a judgment on the changes in the Church, but I'm not surprised at the idea of change in itself. I am really very well impressed by some of the changes, such as those of the Liturgy. That is an excellent procedure, to make the worship of the Church something in which the people can participate more fully.

"And it is certainly high time for more social mindedness, for the Church to express far more concern for the people. That has been a long time coming, and I think it is right that we should see so much of it now. Thirdly, my main impression at first sight, is that the Church has become much more mission minded, much more aware of the other countries of the world and less provincial in its outlook."

The bishop's face grows more serious, and he looks almost quizzically at me as though I might have an answer to the questions he is about to raise. They are obviously important to him, a challenge of sorts to the faith which he has lived so fully and without hesitation for all his days. "Along with all that, I read a lot of alarming news in the daily paper. It is disturbing and alarming to read of crime waves and of the increase in drugs. You know, even with all the opium we had in China, we never had anything like that. To learn that life is unsafe in the cities, that was just amazing to me. When I lived in New York, the police department was one of the best-organized in the world and it kept order everywhere . . ." He pauses as though trying to find an explanation for the strangely changed world to which he came when he left prison in China, "Have the police changed? It was such a marvelous organization. I knew many of the men, including the famous detective, Johnny Broderick. He could settle anything . . ."

Somehow the complexities of modern life have raised questions for Bishop Walsh, but it is a little easier for him to ask about the old metropolitan staples like the police department than it is about the changing priesthood. It is as though he used the reference to the police as an introduction to a subject about which he has a deep feeling.

"I know that many priests are leaving the priesthood. It is just a plain mystery to me how anybody can be a priest and decide to leave; he ought to have his head examined." He does not speak judgmentally but rather in genuine wonderment that such a thing could come to be. "I could understand it out of weakness. I would pity any priest who left for that reason, but, you know, God made us that way and I could understand it. In order to handle our weakness we have to pray, be discreet in our conduct, and use the sacraments regularly. We ought to have the brains enough to take the means that God gave us and handle our life.

Temptation is not surprising in itself, but we ought to learn how to handle it." The bishop is becoming personal for the first time in our interview. "I was so naïve as a young priest about all these things. I thought that with saying Mass and receiving Communion every day that there wouldn't be any temptations at all. I was surprised when I had some myself, and I went to confession. So the priest said to me, 'You're too simple-minded about these things.' And I said to him, 'Well, I didn't know what to make of it.' And he said, 'God doesn't take that away. Say your prayers and avoid the occasions of temptation.'"

He is laughing at his own innocence but he is trying to show that he can understand the temptations men have; it is only in the terminology of temptation that his faith allows him to speak about the possibility of people leaving the priesthood. "So I did say my prayers and I did try to avoid occasions, and I have had very little trouble ever since. I think most of these priests who have left had a vocation and lost it somehow. That's a simple enough thing to do. The greatest tragedy during my years as a superior was that men left the priesthood and I could not help them sufficiently." He is speaking with the deepest feeling of the afternoon now, revealing something that has been on his mind a long time. "The whole time I was in prison one of my chief occupations was to pray for the men who had left the priesthood when I was Superior General."

It is as though he were still shouldering the burden of responsibility which the conception of the superior's role in the old Church had placed on his shoulders. It had been a heavy one indeed for this gentle man. "The first question I asked when I got out of prison and arrived in Hong Kong was about those men who had left. I greatly rejoiced to know that the Church had seen fit to straighten out their illicit marriages." He pauses for a long moment of feeling. "It was the greatest relief I had ever known in my whole life. It had been my chief anxiety all through the years. I cannot tell you how much that meant to me." He sounds relieved again as he recalls his feelings, and he smiles at the fact that he no longer needs to worry and pray about such a responsibility. "Also, I still pray for my troubled people in Shanghai, for all those I knew and loved there."

There is an interval of silence as he thinks back on those years and the puzzle of priests departing from the Church which haunted him and, to some degree, obviously motivated him to pray and suffer for these men during his years of captivity. He changes the subject to the sacramental aspect of faith and, in a tone of some surprise that he should find himself talking about this, says, "I don't know what the most important part of the faith is. As far as that goes, I suppose it is the Blessed Sacrament to bolster our faith and strengthen all the virtues. You know, for twelve years I couldn't receive the Blessed Sacrament. I begged them to send down to the Jesuit Church which wasn't far away, but the officer who denied the permission just couldn't do anything about it. I wasn't allowed to have any religious books either so I prayed from morning until night. I said a dozen rosaries each day. I have always known a lot of prayers, and I have always been very fond of them. I enjoyed it. At last, I felt, I could say all the prayers I wanted to. I was able to have a prayer life all day every day. I used to think to myself: this is my Trappist monastery. I really wasn't unhappy, although I felt the confinement some. I have always felt that God would sustain me in life and that he would see me through that. If it was his will, then it was okay by me. God got me there, and I felt he would also get me out. I had some rough moments, that's true, but I was generally content and happy most of the time . . ."

His profound simplicity is very moving as the afternoon sun disappears and his own strength seems to wane a little. "One additional factor was important. That was, that I wasn't in solitary confinement. I had at least one companion most of the time I was in prison and that was a great consolation to me. One was a young lawyer and a professor. Another was a professor in the senior middle school, something like our junior college. Another was a clerk. They were all university graduates and my association with them meant a lot. Each taught me something about his specialty, and I tried to teach them something about mine.

"The Chinese provided me with other reading matter, plenty of it, although a good bit of it was propaganda mixed up with the news. But there was a lot of ordinary literature, a whole volume of Shakespeare, works of Jules Verne, Gorki, Chekhov, four of Dickens' best novels," he is speaking as one remembering a great feast and time enough to enjoy it. "I remember all that distinctly. Better still, they loaned me one big Chinese dictionary with eight thousand characters in it. It was the standard work. I could spend hours every day delving into that. We all got up at six with the government broadcast and had to take calesthenics, just a few simple gymnastics. Everybody did that and then we would wash. There was good provision for that. We had cold taps and had our own wash basins. You couldn't take a proper bath each day, of course. So we would take what we called a bird bath. Once a week we were allowed to take a bath in the laundry vats. It was a very good provision, something like taking a bath in a tub. There was a regular routine for the rest of the day. We had housekeeping to do, although they wouldn't let me do much of that. Then they would take us up on the roof; it was a flat roof which you could walk on for a half hour every day. Sometimes they would show a motion picture or a propaganda report of some kind, and sometimes they would let us even see TV. That was mostly propaganda too, but occasionally there were acrobats or a ballet. The Chinese are very clever. They can learn anything. I remember seeing the ballet, *Swan Lake* while I was there . . . It was done to perfection.

"If it hadn't been for my belief in God, the Church, and my priesthood, I would have been disconsolate. I remember thinking God's will is good enough for me . . ." His voice trails off. He has not spoken bitterly or harshly but rather as a man whose faith has enabled him to see many years of imprisonment as a kind of a blessing, an opportunity for responding in the way for which his faith had well prepared him. I ask him what is the most important part of the faith for him now.

"I don't know what I could single out. There is such a marvelous treasury of goodness in the Church. My own favorite devotions are to the Sacred Heart and to the Blessed Mother. I can never stop thinking of these two devotions. Others wouldn't feel that way; some would want to have devotion to the Holy Spirit, but these two really fill me up . . ." What, I ask him, would he like the young priests of the world to believe in? "I would want them to believe firmly whatever they believe, and I would want them to carry it out with some practical action for God's people. I do think that is really what is important. God put us in this world to help each other, and we've got to spend our lives in helping each other. That's what God wants and that's all he wants. He's our Father and he has a very big family . . ."

III

WHAT DO I BELIEVE?

FAITH AND LIFE

If believing is a central and integrating human response—one through which we know ourselves and our world—what is it that people believe about? In interviewing many people besides those mentioned in the previous chapters it became clear that the hunger for belief is pervasive and intense, if sometimes unrecognized for what it is. Most people do not identify their own personal searching for the right kind of life as explicitly religious activity, and not often as an aspect of theological faith. They are, even the most sophisticated among them, somewhat unselfconscious in their operational everyday believing. Believing is important to them as individuals and they also understand that no society can rise or stand for long without it, but active human believing seems to them of a different order from belief in God and supernatural truths. Human believing helps you make it through the night, or at least the darker hours of life, but it is often perceived as something that exists in and between persons and is distinct from the kind of religious faith that is described in catechisms and lettered into creeds. People live by what they style a secular faith, but they are saved by a different kind of Faith—a capital letter phenomenon whose source is in God.

Although there are some theologians and other persons of common sense who have come to identify these experiences of faith as different dimensions of the same thing, the boundary line between them remains fairly rigid and fixed in our common way of speaking and teaching. This is part of the heritage of a divided model of man and the universe as well as a failure to understand that we have only our own language and experience with which to speak about our relationship to each other and to God. Rather than raise an argument about why this is so, let us face the fact that we are still far from preaching clearly or in a popular way about the possible coextensive reality of faith in man and faith in God. Perhaps in the everyday lives of those to whom our preaching is addressed sufficient understanding of this already exists, even though it has not yet been formulated into words. When we look at believing persons, at those people who identify themselves clearly as religious believers, many of them already have an unnamed sense about the real depth of their human expressions and exchanges of faith. They recite the creed, of course, and were they asked about the content of their faith, they would point to the teachings of their Church. Despite that, ordinary persons do not determine their lives on the basis of such doctrines as the Trinity. They are affected by creedal statements, especially insofar as these illumine their sense of values, but the countdown to their most important yea's and nay's is marked off on the edges of human experience, on what they have learned to believe about each other in the course of their growth through time.

When we speak about the *sensus fidelium,* the sense of the faithful, we may be referring to this powerful intuition about the rightness or wrongness of certain behaviors or activities that seems to flow out of the bones of the believing community. These judgments, to which we so often turn when theological reasoning fails, are total human responses, the feeling of the group that flows from faith that has become a rich alloy of human experience. When the Christian community, after proper reflection, speaks on some issue, it does not do it in syllogisms. The reaction is closer to poetry than logic because it represents people drawing on resources deep within them and their life histories. The teaching of faith and human experience that is faithful to its own truth do not contradict each other. The average person reacts on the level of what strikes him as right or wrong, quite unconscious of the way faith and experience have been forged into one thing in this judgment. Faith speaks comfortably in a human voice, in tones that reflect a tested capacity to trust mature human reactions to life.

There are others who build a life-style on dogmatic absolutes, threading their way through the human condition by weighing the eternal consequences of each action or decision along the way. The dogmas of heaven or hell are very real to these people as sources of motivation for everything they do from loving their neighbor to keeping the Sabbath. Such persons may go through life hearing the music of heavenly choirs or the crackling of flames, but they are not like most ordinary persons who struggle along with not much more than crowd noises in the background. The individual who regards everything in view of its eternal merits or demerits may obscure his or her view of life to such an extent that they never do quite understand what it is all about. Looking at life in terms of its extrinsic rewards makes it difficult to appreciate its intrinsic meaning. It is no secret that fundamentalistic faith has harbored a traditional distrust and dislike for a great many ordinary life experiences which are counted by most other common people as playful and profoundly human. Such, for example, are courtship, eating and drinking, the use of leisure, and other similar experiences. For the common run of us, these are judged in the context of our overall lives, in terms of what we ourselves mean rather than in terms of what these things, independent of our response, might mean in themselves. To live a life based on selected elements of a creed closes people to great portions of their experience and, therefore, to primary sources of faith.

To approach living faith on the level of what goes on and why it goes on in people's lives may seem theologically naïve. We may, however, understand beliefs better in terms of man's questions than in terms of cut and dried answers. A reciprocal relationship exists between human experience and its reflection in a theological view of life, a continuing dialogue between what persons know together and what the poetic language of faith attempts to identify and to put into perspective for them. This is a living process that allows for growth both in the person's capacity to believe and in his capacity to translate that experience into the language of faith. Man's longings and wonders incorporate him into a life where believing is a functional human response that opens him to all of God's reality by awakening him to the reality he shares with his neighbor.

What are the basic questions that the everyday believer raises and, by so doing, involves himself necessarily with God? These are the recurrent human inquiries that concern men and women everywhere. It is to these questions that any religious faith or philosophy of life must give some explanatory response. Perhaps the best test of any belief system lies in whether it addresses itself to these questions and with what sensitivity it throws light on the human experience that prompts them in the first place. Faith explains; it does not make things more mysterious. It makes it possible for us to live in and with our experience more honestly. It does this in effective language and symbol or it is talking to somebody other than the human person.

The important questions in life hold no surprises for any of us, unless we have come late to be concerned about or to understand them. Life is not a child's garden of verses and a sweet and oversimplified faith, much as we might long for it, does an eventual disservice to man as well as to the capacity of religious faith to explain a sometimes cruel and contradictory world. Religious faith is made for tough, human questions rather than for those that are as fragile and sugary as baker's cookies. In proposing the following themes from common questions I am raising the issues that man wants to know about, that he wants and needs to understand more deeply in order to live more purposefully. Man needs to believe in something in order to answer these satisfactorily; he also needs the explanatory and supportive help of a sensitive religious belief system in order to speak the *credo* that defines his life.

What is existence all about? That is a question that floats near the surface of humanity's consciousness almost all of the time. It is repeated in poems and popular songs as well as in the penny catechism. This subject is debated intellectually, but it rises from deep within the person and abstract and philosophical responses are seldom adequate. The average man is not sustained very much by the notion that life is accidental or ultimately meaningless. He has an inner urge to make sense out of his experience, to find his way through the debris of history, and to glimpse some vision that holds it all together and provides some explanation for the juxtaposed cruelties and joys of being alive. People need to believe something about what they know and feel together that acknowledges the difficulty of getting the pieces of life to fit even approximately into place.

Hard religious questions have echoed in man's consciousness all through history. When the grand design is beyond him he must dig for significance within the restrictions of his own life and occupation. Despite the changes over the centuries, one must wonder whether the person with the routine job who makes his way to and from his Bronx apartment every day has a clearer view of ultimate meanings than the factory worker in Dickens' London or the farmer battling the seasons on the frontier. No person wants to believe that he is insignificant, a grain of sand indistinguishable from the shifting dune. Men and women have always ached for a sense of something that supports the meaning of their anonymous lives, and they often find it in the midst of their relationships with each other. Meaning in general can only dawn for the individual who experiences specific meaning with another person; the very notion of meaning is otherwise only an abstraction. It is in each other's company that common believers begin the search for the difficult questions of why they are alive; it is from the qualities that inhere in what they experience together that they sense throughout themselves the meaning of believing. Just as an infant's introduction to life depends on his first experiences of trust, so our further entrance into practical believing rests on an ever-maturing experience of what it means to be believed in by somebody else and what it means to believe in them in return. Man can believe in his larger meaning—and in an evolving destiny that makes sense out of all creation—only when he has tasted the experience of believing in relationship to another human being. This is a fundamental transaction which God does not by-pass in giving us the gift of faith. We are prepared to understand the world and a faithful God as its creator if we have first stood on the foundations for this in life with others. The kind of believing we do in each other is the beginning of the believing we experience in God; God is believable to those who have known believable persons. We give each other hints and intuitions of the depths of God's concern and faithfulness through our faithfulness to each other. The believing response, which is in itself integrative of our world of meaning, cannot be divided up; it is one thing, and the more fully it is experienced with our fellow men the more clearly it shades into a deeper sense of God's goodness and presence.

Meaning is never yielded once and for all, no matter how eager the inquirer nor how profound his personal experience of meaning in communion with other persons. Meaning does not come in chunks, but as an emerging pattern whose main lines not only fit but extend what we have understood before. Our experiences of believing give us a sense of direction and a center of gravity that allow us to pursue meaning more deeply. Scenes shift, of course, even in the realm of our human experience. This is so because human beings grow and find that their perspective necessarily changes as they develop. New awarenesses come, uncharted weaknesses are stumbled upon, and unsuspected sources of strength are also uncovered. Only a believer who understands that this is a dynamic process can grow old with some sense that he is on a journey that has an ultimate meaning. He changes his notions about this meaning as he passes through various life stages, and he can only do this successfully if, in a very real sense, he keeps faith with his transforming self. A person is called on not only to believe in his possibilities but also to respond to his actualities; that is, to keep bringing forth what is true of himself in the face of a wide variety of challenges and difficulties. A faithfulness to the truth of one's person—which, of course, involves us in fidelity to those around us—means that we refine an essential sense of ourselves that remains constant and deepens as time passes. That reliable core is what we recognize as trustworthy in each other; it also enables us to believe in an essentially responsive and faithful God. As we explore the depths of ourselves, in other words, we find the experience that allows us gradually to understand something of God himself. The sense of meaning that emerges from this experience is not easily defined because it cannot be summed up rationally, and it is not just something in the realm of emotions. It is in the order of personal experiencing, the way we understand on several levels what it means to belong to a family, or to be in love. Believing—and reaching out for meaning—are the kinds of thing we do with the wholeness of ourselves. Belief is predicated of the person, not just of the intellect or of the heart. When a person says, "I believe . . ." he says something about what he does in and through the complex unity of his personality; he also acknowledges overall meanings that are best described in the special language of symbols.

Believing forever involves us in questions not because of some human reluctance to believe but because it is through questions that we make our way forward into the deeper waters of existence. In order to believe more firmly an individual must constantly test the explanations delivered to him on the fine edge of his life experience. Only the somnolent believer fails to ask questions, and that is an indication that believing no longer sends out strong signals inside him. Settling for security, which is the death of inquiry, has always meant the end of active believing. Security ends disturbing thoughts, of course, and excuses us from examining our motives or recasting our religious symbols, but it also blows out the flame of living faith. In fact, it imposes a deadness on life's best invitations that is hardly made up for by the seeming stability of an unquestioning acceptance of any one set formula of faith or explanation of life. The trouble with being a believer, it turns out, is that security is always being surrendered in view of living in a fuller and richer way.

Perhaps an analogy with a recent development in the institution of marriage will help; the problems are, in fact, not dissimilar. Some couples, in order to effect equality of relationship and to avoid the misunderstandings and other contingencies of living together, draw up elaborate contracts stating each party's rights and obligations. The contract settles most of the problems that plague less-precise arrangements. Security based on justice insures a kind of stability that minimizes the chances of hurt. In marriages where a man and woman sincerely build their relationship on faith associated with love, such a contract would seem out of place. They know that they give up a measure of stability by committing themselves to each other in a relationship that is fundamentally unpredictable. Its stability, however, is of another sort, quite different from that of a legally binding contract. It is built on belief in each other, the kind of commitment that strengthens us and makes us vulnerable at the same time. A couple who want to grow in their love know that they cannot shut themselves off from questions nor from the experiences of change that are bound to occur because of illness, aging, or other processes. They live by a kind of faith that is enhanced by the explorations of self that are demanded of a man and woman who must continually find new answers together. They experience life through their belief in each other and through their willingness to risk change and hurt in pursuit of greater truth and depth together. It is the same way for the questioning believer; the search keeps him alive and responsive even though it asks him to live on the quivering edge of doubt and self-exploration.

Many persons do not formalize their day-to-day difficulties in terms of generalized theological questions; they must deal with them on the level at which they meet them and give the best answers they can. It is difficult for most hardworking people to get very far in self-reflection or to draw much consolation or insight from the prophetic arts. They are too up against mortgages, sick children, and self-doubt to do much more, in the welter of everyday activity, than the best they can with the hope and prayer that it is the right thing. This rather general state of affairs makes the challenge and opportunity of organized religion all the more significant. The Churches are meant to supply the symbols and rituals that cut across the fatigue and confusion of life to deliver redemptive meaning to ordinary persons. The marvelous work of organized religion is to provide the environment of active faith that speaks in many languages beyond that of logic of the religious significance and value of living. In a sense, the Churches have the role of wise and skilled counselors who know how to listen to even the slightest cry or least aspiration of human hearts and to respond with the words, images, liturgies, and relationships that say, in effect, "You and your life are understandable; what you long for makes sense. Read and recognize the story of your life in what the Lord teaches. Takes strength from his promises." Churches do not, in other words, preach or celebrate things that take people away from their struggles; they proclaim the religious reality of what people already experience. This is the kind of lively faith that makes it possible for persons whose lives may be splintered by a thousand cares to see themselves whole again. Such a living faith also underscores the moments and the values of existence that are truly redemptive.

The average person keeps faith by bringing himself as honestly and truly as he or she can to the mostly undramatic but steadily demanding problems of living. The Church, much as it does in witnessing the reality of marriage in the promises man and woman make to each other, constantly witnesses the saving realities of everyday life, pointing to and celebrating the incidents of trial and growth, the deaths and resurrections, through which we redeem ourselves and each other. The basic themes of the ordinary life have always existed; Jesus preaches their deepest meaning in his words and life. He reveals the profundity of our existence for us. We are strangers no more because we now possess the Spirit to illumine the faith meaning of being human. The true impulse of Church renewal is to draw back together the substance of life and faith, to make existence whole again by proclaiming the unity of our human and spiritual experience. The average person's test of belief has always been how he lives rather than how distinctly he recites the articles of the creed. There is, in other words, something always unconscious and unsymbolized about the lives of believers. They do not always know quite what they are doing, except that they are trying to do what is true and right. Just as the best kind of love is that which is unstudied and spontaneous, so the best kind of belief is not planned but comes to life in the moments that call for faithfulness and fidelity, for being responsive to the best possibilities in ourselves and in others. Formal faith helps us to recognize the deeper meaning of our homely efforts to invest ourselves truthfully in life; it validates them and strengthens us to continue giving our best to the unfolding mystery of our own incarnation.

Most people are so pressed with immediate concerns that they do not think very clearly or in much detail about whether they are being faithful or religious in dealing with these difficulties. Often enough, the persons who are self-consciously religious—pious might be a better word—destroy their own capacity for spontaneity and take the living quality out of what they call faith. Such, for example, are the do-gooders who are nice to you, not so much because of yourself but because they profess to see Christ in you. This is the

classic illustration of behaving religiously in the best ways
for the wrong reasons. Faith is not something conjured up to
justify responding to persons in need; it inheres in the very
response we make to the needy around us. We are faithful
when we make ourselves present for the sake of others rather
than for an invented reason that makes faithfulness extrinsic to human experience. People need the confirmation of
their best instincts that religion affords as it puts into italics
the experiences that are genuinely redemptive. Religion
does not add redemptive meaning to these; it recognizes
and celebrates it where it truly is.

The average individual may be more aware of his needs
than anything else. Life consists in getting through the activities and demands of the day with at least some minimal
sense that it means something. It includes doing a decent
job, being sensitive to one's family, and following the dictates of one's conscience. It extends to wanting to be loved
and trying to love at the same time, of wanting to be fair
and to be treated fairly as well. Each day can be like every
other one unless faith identifies those human exchanges in
which we, in fact, work out our salvation together. People
acquire a certain measure of wisdom, knowing, for example,
that other people can hurt you, that they can be mean and
small, and that even those you love can disappoint you. Average men live with debts and taxes, with things they cannot control, and problems they wish that they did not have
to pay any attention to. They are surrounded at times by
cruelties and injustices, by multiplied unfairnesses that
make them wonder more than ever just what life, with bro-
ken promises and sudden deaths, with loose ends and unful-
filled hopes, really is all about.

It is in lives where persons are clearly aware of these problems that faith is already a living reality. The more an individual is committed to other persons, to achieving certain
honorable goals, or to improving the world in some way, the
more that individual must be an active believer. Faith is
something like the soul of life, the animating and energizing

quality that makes existence possible and meaningful. The capacity to believe processes experience, enabling persons to reach each other, develop communities, and to enlarge man's sense of his own spirit and destiny. It is activated in all the difficult circumstances of life where gaps seem to exist in reasonableness and justice, in those incidents where evil abounds and the person is treated shamefully. Believing is the only response adequate to the constant sacrileges committed against humanity. It is what men and women must do against all odds in order to give birth to a new and better future. Faith has a creative function for the person, because through it he can renew himself and others even in the most desperate of situations.

Because men and women must believe—must, in other words, keep committing themselves to some framework of meaning in order to survive—the content of that framework is crucial. Man believes but what he believes is decisive about the quality of his life or the depth of his achievements. If, for example, men's beliefs are so diluted that they barely nourish or encourage him, he will have a difficult time facing up to the difficult questions that parade before him in the course of life. If the person is nothing but an intricate machine, if all there is to believe in is efficiency, pleasure, or taking care of oneself, then belief itself is as restricted as a dove with taped wings; it cannot even feel its power or its possibilities. That is why it is so important to associate religious faith with the richest possibilities of human personality. In a very real sense, the content of religious faith must help the person to believe in his own possibilities, to see past his faults to the self-transcending experiences of which he is capable. That is one of the extraordinary aspects of the teachings of Jesus. He tells men and women, for example, that they can rise above the vindictiveness and estrangement that fill their lives when they do not keep faith with each other. He says there are yet resources of healing and self-realization that can be called upon if a person believes deeply enough. The content of the Christian Gospel bids man always to go deeper into himself and his experience, to find the kingdom within himself, in the powers that he can draw on to become his best self. That is not the power of positive thinking but the much harder task of finding and bringing the undiscovered aspects of our identity into being. Only a faith whose content recognizes and symbolizes the fact that the person can always find fuller life—only that faith can ever make him whole.

Faith is intimately involved in the human story, and religious faith takes us more deeply into it rather than farther out of it. The eyes of faith permit us to see ourselves as we are—and the selves we can yet be. It is the spark that dances across these flash points of experience all the days of our lives. Faith, then, is far from a frozen set of dogmas, and it has little resemblance to wishful thinking. Faith, in so far as it organizes us and orients us to what is really happening in and around us, situates us in reality rather than in some escapist delusions about life. First of all, faith roots us in time, in that strange indefinable experience that can be alternately perceived as an enemy or a friend. Faith does not merely espy the timeless world to come; it does something quite different because it alerts us to our meaning in time, rather than just outside of it. Faith, in a certain sense, confronts us with time as an unalterable and yet profound condition of our self-realization and redemption. As psychologist Henri Yaker has observed:

> Men are called to redeem the contents of life *in life*, to salvage life by working in time until the final time, to find meaning by making each hour of life a theo-temporal hour, through decision rather than relying upon a cosmic transformation of nature. Not to be found in wind, hurricanes, and storms, Yahweh is to be found in history, where men can read the beginning by the end, rather than the other way around.[1]

[1] "Time in the Biblical and Greek Worlds" in *The Future of Time*, Yaker, Osmond, Cheek, eds., (Garden City: Anchor Books, Doubleday & Company, Inc., 1972), p. 33.

Believing activity, in other words, involves us in ransoming our own time constantly through our acceptance of it as the medium in and through which we sense and touch each other's lives. Faith forces us to deal with time and it never excuses us from this task. No mystical vision of eternity nor of a world beyond time was ever granted to anyone who was not first of all clearly anchored in his or her own time or age. Faith, the act through which we make ourselves present to reality as it is and we are, provides the basis for the other rich and complex responses through which we best respond to time as a condition of life. These are, of course, hope and love, each of which enables us to deal with the temporal condition of our lives in a constructive manner. Through hope and love we do, in fact, redeem our times by operationally living out the vision of meaning and values supplied by faith. Believing inserts us in meaningful time because it lights up the significance of the human community and builds the foundations for the experiences through which we touch each other's lives redemptively. Faith alters our time sense; it does not just manipulate or distort it the way a drug might. We experience time more fully because we see the world and ourselves more clearly by the light of its revelation. *Now* is the time of salvation, the Bible tells us, and so it is for the believer who understands that only as we enter into the demanding processes that take their shape in time that we lay hold of our deepest sense of personal meaning. The believer becomes a hoper and a lover in the gritty world of time and space. That is where we sense the mysteries with which we must deal if we are going to be true believers.

These include the strange mystery of ourselves, for example, and the many layers of our experience which we must befriend in some way before we can possess or become ourselves. The problem is that we need a sense of our own possibilities of growth, a vision of what we can become, if we are going to face the complex and ambivalent strands of our own identity. Faith provides that vision because it acknowledges the roiling primitive qualities within us while it enables us to temper and integrate these as part of our true selves. That is how faith makes us whole, by making it possible for us to face the evil inside of us and not to be overcome by it. The men or women who remain unacquainted with the dark side of themselves are strangers to their real identity. Belief has the power to fuse these complex energies so that they may serve rather than betray the unique individual personality.

Faith gives us a good look at ourselves when its dimensions of potential meaning are large and strong enough to accept the human personality in all its flawed majesty. Any vision of supposed faith that deliberately truncates or automatically rules out certain parts of our experience harms man more than it helps him. Such, as psychologist Rollo May has noted, are the images of the noble savage or the totally good young who can only be corrupted from the outside. This generates what May terms a pseudo-innocence because such individuals never identify or come to terms with the other very real and very powerful aspects of their personality. They fail to achieve that identity that is based on their complex internal reality; they do not know how to use aggression or other strong feelings constructively. Their faith in themselves, their fellow man, and God is restricted because they have neither seen nor understood the full truth about themselves.

Faith serves an integrating function because it does not flinch at what it finds in our ambivalence or narcissistic self-concern. It provides us with the view of reaching beyond these, using their strengths for the richer purposes of serving and loving others. The person who is faithful to himself has power—the power of the Spirit—to harness his passions positively. He can believe in himself because he is not surprised at himself, and he knows that his development is never perfect nor finished with. He must keep believing, in other words, to keep himself together in a healthy dynamic way; his believing sums himself up, good and bad, in a discernible identity. That, of course, is the kind of person in whom others can also believe, in whom they spontaneously believe because he is already available to them in a rich and true manner. Deceit, defensiveness, the manipulation of appearances: All of these are used to get a response from people. They may get a species of acquiescence, a shallow response, but it is nothing like the kind of faith we invest in people who are trustworthy precisely because their faults—and therefore their depths—are not hidden.

This life-oriented belief allows persons to deal with their guilt as well as the myriad uneasinesses that accompany us through life. The achievement of healthy self-esteem depends on establishing a truthful relationship to ourselves. If we are horrified by the discoveries we make about our capacities to fall short of an ideal, we will never be comfortable with or confident in ourselves. The faith that understands man enables him to face and forgive himself for the jumbled psychological inheritance within. It is precisely this shambling and faulted self that we must believe in if we are going to live what we call the Christian life. We confront ourselves as sinners—or at least as psychologically imperfect—and we can begin to do something in and through this true personality of ours. We are, in a brief definition, believing sinners who through faith find the strength to forgive and heal and love. That is what the life of faith is all about—redeeming ourselves through the promises Jesus gave us when he took on the human condition.

The process aspect of living faith—the way this is accomplished—involves us in something we would avoid completely if we were terrorized by our shortcomings. The central, mystical, and transforming experience of faith asks us to let others see the truth of ourselves, to reveal, in other words, precisely what we are afraid people will find out— who and what we really are. The dynamic, as mentioned in an earlier chapter, places us at that point of necessary convergence between what has been called natural and supernatural faith. The processes are indistinguishable and can be recognized as aspects of the same thing in those moments when we believe enough in ourselves and others to let them see us as we are. This transaction changes us, exorcising the demons within by taking away their selfish destructive power, and allowing us to become more of our true selves at the same time. It is also a reciprocal process because, as we reveal ourselves, so the other responds with a greater revelation of his or her truth as well. People have to believe in each other in order to enter into this experience—and they deepen their belief through the process itself. We know even as we are known in the experience that allows us some insight into the faithful person's dynamic and reciprocal relationship with God. Knowing and being known counterpoint the faith experience of life, allowing us to deal with our tangled personal truths, to redeem and give wholeness to each other, and to sense the reality beyond us of which these are image and echo.

CREATIVE FAITH

Creeds are easy, unless you are a philosopher who ago-nizes over the working of a particular clause. The recital of the creed gives us a sense of security and makes us feel comfortable and approved by the Church itself. We are so habituated to the doctrinal summation through a lifetime of repetition that we may be dulled to the more exciting and confronting aspects of living faith. I do not believe that you can make an act of faith in the mysteries of the God-head in other than a living and changing manner. We are the ones who live and change, of course, and our faith is constantly shifting and expanding in order to accommodate the pressures of its own developing complexity. William James, the famous psychologist, once said that we believe all that we can and would believe everything if we only could. The person is a believer but not in a naïve or easy manner; as he matures he must believe more and take more risks and more deep breaths in the process. As we grow older we find that life is not exactly what we thought it was, and although we may therefore feel betrayed, we can neither turn back nor look away without betraying our-selves even more. Believing makes adults out of us when we have to search our reservoir of faith for the understand-ings and symbols to explain wickedness, tragedy, and the failure of love. This does not require us to hold on to a child's version of the universe but actively to search out an adult's understanding of it.

This is the part that is difficult because, quite against our expectation that religious faith will calm our inner seas, we discover that it leads us into brisker winds and more towering storm clouds. Faith does not pull us apart but neither does it set us apart from what all men and women must face once they awaken to the mysterious challenges of becoming human. These include many elements, from the loss of their first innocence about the sun-filled world of childhood to the last tasks of old age in which life, like an unbraiding rope, can seem to come apart before they have even had a good look at it. The developing person becomes more aware of his or her own complexity through all of this, especially in the area of human relationships that seem to be self-entangling and almost too painful to speak the truth about. This sense of a differentiated and non-simple self is further weighted with a sense of the dreams and longings we have shared with all those who have lived before us and who, in some way, seem to live in us still. How does a person get enough room even to see himself clearly for a moment, much less to grasp his own or the world's meaning?

A simple and old-fashioned faith may seem the right answer to the questions without answers that gradually pile up in the minds of sensitive persons. This works for some, although it is not certain that they are more blessed because of that. Such a faith may shut their eyes against the landscape of life so that they do not know its terrors, but they miss its beauty as well. Believing persons need a religious faith that opens them to, even when it cannot fully explain, the contradictions and sometimes non-linear quality of human experience. Believing is more like sailing on uncharted seas than staying in port telling tales of the demons over the horizon. Sailing is not a glass-sea sport; only the individual ready to harness the invisible wind can ride the cauldron successfully. Faith does not make the journey easy; it does, however, make it possible and, at each succeeding stage, meaningful. I believe, in other words, that religious faith is made for living life rather than for hiding away from it. It must, therefore, be capable of sustaining us as we grow, become puzzled, hurt, and finally transformed by the whirling and flashing experiences of life.

Faith is not a preservative; it does not fix explanations that last, in any one form, for a lifetime. Faith is something alive, a dynamic that relates us to the shifting nature of ourselves and our world. It is creative of ourselves and of our individual meaningful experience of life. Believing involves us in a process that is endlessly repeated for each of us and is never fully completed for any of us. The essential notes of what it means to believe are best understood if we look at the creative process itself. This helps to illumine what I believe in about belief and also allows us to appreciate the manner in which we know deep within us the basic rhythm of the Christian view of life.

This catches what Jesus meant when he spoke of our need to have the faith of little children. It is the unspoiled vision of the child that must be available to the creative person if he is to break out of a prefabricated existence and bring something new into the world. The child has a vision of *the possible* about things; this is the same vision the creative person employs as he or she looks at a problem or works toward a deeper insight. The vision of *the possible* is precisely what faith restores to us so that we can, in fact, get up in the morning, or return to tasks and relationships which would otherwise break us under their deadening and totally predictable weight. This refocus on the possible—on all that is fresh and yet to be—is a healthy impulse through which we let go of something of ourselves in order to lay hold of something richer and better. The basic experience of the creative artist of any kind involves him in a dying to himself in order to bring a new vision of the possible into existence. This is not something that the creative person can plan or induce; it is in the order of response to what he or she can see in life. Believing is just such an experience because it continually challenges us to look at life and, even at the price of death to an old way of looking at things, to respond with behavior that springs from the level of possibility rather than cliché. That cannot be planned, and it is only faintly memorialized by reciting various creeds; it is something demanding a reorganization of ourselves in accordance with a lively vision rather than a happy memory.

Poets speak of learning to "throw themselves away" in the creative process, of having to surrender themselves in order to bring an enlarged self to life. They experience a certain disorganization of their adjustment in view of this newer and higher level of integration. They suffer what psychologist Frank Barron has called an experience of "diffusion" in order to be able to come together again in the achievement of their creation. They re-create themselves, one might say, even as the believer, facing the changing and difficult contours of his experience, must, in the very act of believing, disorganize himself and bring himself together around the vision of possibilities that his faith makes available to him. This is the way in which faith makes us whole, not by cementing us in some former set toward life, but by breaking us open continuously so that we can be reintegrated at a higher level with a deepened sense of ourselves and of the meaning of our lives. This is the mystic realm of religious experience, and it has a face as plain and simple as everyday life in which we die daily, not through stoic mortification but through creative living.

The very word *creative* has been cheapened in our culture and it may be difficult to grasp it again as the most profoundly descriptive word that we have about the life of faith. That is why we work out our salvation in fear and trembling rather than in safety and security; the creative strength of believing is manifest in the conditions of uncertainty and ambivalence that mark our days. We are meant to respond to each other on the risky edge of living where only those with a vision of the possible are capable of giving new life to each other. As Frank Barron notes, in his description of the creative artist's work:

. . . the individual is willing to "die unto himself," i.e., to permit an achieved adaptation or state of relative equilibrium to perish. And there are not guarantees that something better will thereby be arrived at. Looking backwards from the end point of the creative process, we are inclined to say, "Ah, yes, it had to be so; the chance had to be taken; the chalice could not be passed; the agony was necessary for the redemption and the resurrection." But facing forward in time we see only risk and difficulty, and if we have not the courage to endure diffusion ("suffer death") we cannot achieve the new and more inclusive integration ("gain the light").[1]

The ordinary person is immersed in a life that asks him to be creative in his own way, to leave his mark not on a statue or a poem but on those he loves or teaches or just stands by in hard times. Creativity for most of us is not taking a ceramics class in evening school as much as it is facing into every day with a vision of its promises and a willingness to die to something of ourselves in order to re-deem these. The psychological reality of the process is lighted up by, but not radically different from, the struggle of the writer or the sculptor. What is striking, of course, is how these dynamics parallel the life theme of all of Jesus' teaching. We are given life not to hoard it nor to protect it but to invest it through committing ourselves, at the risk of suffering, to re-creating the face of the earth. The work of the Spirit is surely that of the faith we profess: to take on our flesh, that is, our own identity, and to suffer the deaths that are the necessary condition for our resurrecting our-selves and others with new life. We keep faith by respond-ing with our total selves to this most fundamental of all religious experiences, the daily round of living and loving that defines life for most of us.

It has always seemed to me that the questioning Nicode-mus, wondering how a man could be born again, was star-

[1] "Diffusion, Integration, and Enduring Attention," in *Study of Lives*, ed. by Robert W. White (New York: Prentice-Hall, 1963), p. 247.

ing, with only a stirring of comprehension, at the possibilities of the faith life that Jesus was preaching to him. "How can a man be born again?" is indeed a profound and bewildering inquiry because it raises the vision that believing in Jesus enables us to re-create ourselves, to return after our failures to a renewed sense of our possibilities with each other. Ordinary life is not supplanted but fulfilled by the regenerating power through which we can meet again after we have injured each other with the creative and redemptive faith that enables us to see what we can be once more. What is Christian forgiveness from the heart if not the restoration of our possibilities? We are continually born again—and not just metaphorically—through our faith in Jesus. That belief enables us to recognize the essential features of life, to see deeply into them as the human raw material of our redemption, much as the artist's creative eye allows him to see deeply into the changing colors of a sunset or the beauty in the tired faces of homeward bound commuters. Faith enables us to see what is already there in a fresh manner and to give our best energies to it every day. We are born again by reaching toward each other across the crooked ways and mounted entanglements of daily life.

Jesus, in responding to Nicodemus, seems to say this clearly as he concludes, ". . . he who acts in truth comes into the light, to make clear that his deeds are done in God." (John 3:21.) Belief in the Lord, in other words, provides the vision of the human situations and responses that are redemptive transactions. Faith lights these up and enables us to recognize the values that are the foundations of the Kingdom. Creative believing always gives life but it is not a sweet or easy exercise. Being born again is a difficult task, and it is only accomplished by those who learn to face the hurts and deaths that are implicit in finding and rooting out what is selfish in ourselves so that our own truth can emerge more clearly. There is a lot of dying in forgiving others or in allowing them to forgive us for the way we can misunderstand and mistreat each other in life. If we could not be born again, if we could not return to a sense of our possibilities—the very thing that creative faith enables us to do—we would be the most desperate of persons. It was well said by Paul that without the power of the Resurrection our faith would be vain and our human state pitiable.

Jesus does not point away from but squarely at our lives as the setting in which we save and are saved through believing. I am indebted to a scripture scholar colleague, John McGovern, a Maryknoll priest now teaching in Guatemala, for a reminder of how directly Jesus draws us back to a sharpened sense of our true selves in Luke's Gospel. Luke 9:51 to 19:28, in what scholar John L. McKenzie has termed the "conscious art" of Luke, is an extended manual for Christian believers. This journey narrative presents Jesus moving into his future, his journey into the *eschaton*, the age of Christ and the age of all Christians. We find powerful insights into the human dimensions of believing stated within this tension-giving setting of Jesus on the way to the accomplishment of his life work. At the very start, four themes emerge which allow us to understand what we must face in ourselves and in life if we are to make the journey of faith with him. We read of four human encounter situations that describe essential characteristics of believing disciples. They underscore rather than override experiences that we can all recognize very clearly:

"These entered a Samaritan town to prepare for his passing through, but the Samaritans would not welcome him because he was on his way to Jerusalem. When his disciples James and John saw this, they said, 'Lord, would you not have us call down fire from heaven to destroy them?' He turned toward them only to reprimand them." (Luke 9:52–56.)

Jesus points to the strength we need to be non-violent in the believing life. This can only arise in the lives of those who have come to terms with themselves and the shadowed side of their personalities. It is easy to hurt and to be vengeful, but it is far more difficult to temper one's hostile impulses in the perspective of a larger and more understanding view of life. The believer, in other words, does not act only on his immediate feelings of the moment because he can see beyond the instant to a broader purpose that is poorly served by anger and the desire to get even. The passage recognizes our human capacity for destructive violence and singles it out as something that must die if we are to re-create the face of the earth.

The follower of Jesus is ever ready, then, to understand and forgive both himself and others, a process that requires more than diplomacy and tact. It demands a steady transformation of ourselves and a willingness to surrender small and easy victories in view of making ourselves present in a truly healing way in life. The believer is not a stranger to his own humanity; he or she has achieved a wholeness that does not naïvely ignore our potential evil but chooses to subordinate and defuse this in view of a more patient and understanding approach to mankind. Violence is one of our easiest temptations; to be determinedly non-violent in order to be understanding is a foundation stone of the unabstracted life of faith.

"As they were making their way along, someone said to him, 'I will be your follower wherever you go.' Jesus said to him, 'The foxes have lairs, the birds of the sky have nests, but the Son of Man has nowhere to lay his head.'" (Luke 9:57–58.)

Jesus points to a central human problem which is related to our capacity to respond creatively in life. The person must find his own center, his or her own substantial identity, as the anchor point in the shifting and insecure environment of life. An individual may listen to many voices within himself—and to many more in the world beyond him—but, in the last analysis, he must live out of his own depths or he fails to live truly at all. The believer, in other words, must examine and test his beliefs against experience, opening rather than closing himself or herself continually to the teeming contradictions of life, not depending on fads or rumors, but on the purified sense of the inner self that is thereby achieved. Our personal identity—knowing who we are as individuals—is, therefore, not a luxury but a prerequisite for the life of faith. We can only believe in and through our own personality or our signature of faith is counterfeit. It is not possible to believe maturely merely on the strength of somebody else's persuasion; that is, of course, the perennial danger attached to enthusiastic but not necessarily very deep religious movements. Faith does not obliterate our identity; rather it builds on it, giving a blessing to every sincere effort to bring the truth of our selves and the richness of our unique gifts into being.

"To another he said, 'Come after me.' The man replied, 'Let me bury my father first.' Jesus to him, 'Let the dead bury their dead; come away and proclaim the kingdom of God.'" (Luke 9:59–60.)

In this passage, frequently moralized into thoughts about filial piety, Jesus points to a deep and abiding issue which the believer must confront and deal with in life. Indeed, it is one of the most difficult problems that can be faced by persons because it centers on the conflict of loyalties that is inevitable in the human situation. The believer must be able to recognize rather than deny the conflicts, many of which are rooted in patterns of life that are self-enclosing. This is true in something as familiar as the merger of separate families through the marriage of two of their members. The clash of traditions and of simple ways of doing things generates tension in many a household. It is very hard for any of us to detach ourselves from our own heritage without disowning it, to make room for another in our life-space without absorbing them totally in our life-style. Selfishness closes us over, making us view the world systematically in terms of our own self-interest. This bony ring of self-concern chokes us to death because, whether in reference to us as individuals, families, or peoples, it convinces us that there is only one way to do something and that is our way. The believer must grow in what psychologist Gordon Allport once described as the process of decentering ourselves. This requires a willingness to die, which leads to the resurrection experience of resolving differences and respecting persons of different backgrounds and outlooks.

The first step in breaking free of our own cramped vision of the universe is the recognition that we will experience tension in admitting and working out the divided loyalties of our lives. It is an on-going process that measures the breadth and depth of our Christian vision. Nobody can escape this sharply honed dimension of personal growth which insistently asks that we discover new possibilities of response and affirmation within ourselves. The believer who does not recognize this as an essential component of the faith response is dealing with a dead rather than a living faith.

"Yet another said to him, 'I will be your follower, Lord, but first let me take leave of my people at home.' Jesus answered him, 'Whoever puts his hand to the plow but keeps looking back is unfit for the reign of God.'" (Luke 9:61–62.)

In an era during which so many persons have acceded to nostalgia for what seems to have been a simpler past, this statement of the Lord's is a forthright and strong invitation to be decisive in the present in view of the future, to live now for the world that is just coming into being. Religious nostalgia is as tempting an invitation as any other form of retrospective longing, and many people, worn down by the strain of renewal and its transformations, wish for a restoration of what were at least more secure good old days.

Jesus challenges any such inclinations with this response which reminds the believer of his essential orientation toward the discovery and creativity of a new age. The person of faith does more than remember or mourn what has gone before. Belief opens us to what can be if we have the courage to let go of our past because of our Christian realization that we are builders of the future. The believing Christian takes on responsibility for his or her decisions, understanding the risk implicit in each one and moving with them toward the future to which they give shape.

Contemporary America is fascinated with the future; nobody is more committed to it than the man or woman of faith who actively attempts to make it a place in which the human family can realize its destiny more fully. B. F. Skinner is absolutely correct in saying that we cannot scare people into preparing for a better future; the Christian vision of the Gospel offers us the sense of direction and the guarantees we need in order to build it in a positive and hopeful manner. That takes a living commitment to things we have not yet seen or heard, to the possibilities of people whose faces we will never see, to the next things more than the last things.

Near the end of the musical play *1776* a discouraged John Adams, having arrived early in the room where the divided colonial delegates have been meeting, steps toward the front of the darkened stage and poses a question to the audience. "Is anybody there? Does anybody care?" he asks plaintively, "Does anybody see what I see?" In many ways, modern man, peering into the darkness of his future, is placing the same questions. Is anybody there? Does anybody care? These are the searching inquiries that make believers examine themselves in terms of the qualities listed by Luke in his narrative. The believer must hear the questions of contemporary men and women and respond with the faith that does not necessarily answer all their wonders but which at least helps to frame them in appropriate human theological terms. The Church stands there, its spires against the darkness, not so much as a symbol of its past as a sign of its living concern for the future. Believing is operative and functional in history but only when believers are alive to their own capacity to breathe on others and to resurrect them, to give them back their possibilities, to give the family of man its future. Is anybody there? Does anybody care? Does anybody see what I see? Only we believers can give the answers to these haunting questions.

WHAT DO I BELIEVE IN?

The question is fair enough if only because I have put it to so many people over the past few months. It is a question that cannot be answered fully in intellectual terms, perhaps not in any terms. Believing is an activity that arises from many levels of our being. Some of these we recognize; others we glimpse only fleetingly; still others we never sense at all. Believing is something we do with all of ourselves; it can never be summed up in intellectual statements alone, howsoever worthy these may be. I think it is relatively easy to recite the creed and to think we have accomplished a religious action. The test of the creed is, however, in life, as it always has been. That is something that involves more than our minds, and we can only explore it with practical theological questions like, "Why do I get up in the morning?" "How do I love my friends and enemies?" and "Why do I live the life that I do?" Something as personal as believing requires personal answers.

I believe in faith as a dynamic process—a living part of ourselves—which is redemptive and creative of life and through which we recognize the religious nature of the adventurous pilgrimage we are on together. Jesus came to point toward those parts of life in which operative faith yields a renewing wholeness of meaning. I believe that the Church is meant to be creative in its own commitment to this living faith and that the last thing it needs to fear is the inevitable dying that is the price of a fuller realization of itself. It is understandable that the Church—or that those who administer it—is keenly aware of its structures and traditions, but these are meant to house a living and sometimes squabbling family of believers rather than an obedient and loyal regiment. Faith, like creative energy, is meant to be expended rather than conserved.

I believe in Jesus, then, not just as a great man nor a distant historical character but as a living presence who reveals both the Father and the meaning of our lives to us. If we examine our lives, I think we can see the experiences through which we redeem ourselves through redeeming each other. We live in a continuing mystery of his own existence and come to face and know for ourselves the great moments of meeting and sharing and separating through which we express the faith that continually recreates and therefore resurrects us. You can feel that in the tensions of being true to yourself that are found not in dramatic incidents but in familiar events, like keeping a promise or being an honest friend or being faithful to somebody we love. Something dies and something new comes to life in us when we make a free and open entrance into these believing moments. They are scattered throughout every day, the raw material of redemption that is processed creatively by living faith.

I believe, therefore, in the Church not as an authoritarian institution with all the answers; it has never been very believable in that guise anyway, nor, for that matter true to itself. The Church does much better by itself and by man when, like the creative person, it "throws itself away" in an ever fresh redemptive commitment to the people of the world. To do this it must allow some of its crustier defenses to die and to reveal its mystery and wisdom more freely. Christ's Church is surely meant to be a creative force rather than a fixative in human history. The remarkable thing is that it has such enormous creative resources at its disposal for accomplishing the primary task of symbolizing and celebrating the central redemptive aspects of life. Instead of treating its human and symbolic wealth gingerly, or with a banker's view to control, the Church can freely spend its resources and only find them recreated as a result.

Many observers have noted that the search for contemporary religious symbols and myths—the very language faith lives on—is one of our most urgent quests. We need to speak to human experience in those symbolic terms and stories that enable the person to find his way through the wasteland and back to a sense of himself. This primarily occurs through the work of creative theologians and liturgists who can sense the religious truths that need to be expressed in fresh ways and who need encouragement and support to do it for us. These are people who, like all true creators, move into the darkness, not self-conscious about their movements but sure of their sense of direction. These creative believers discover and hold up for the rest of us the symbols that bind our faith and experience together. If there was ever a time when we needed healthy creativity in the service of believing man, it is surely now. The temptation, of course, is to keep these people under control lest they disturb something called tradition. A misapplied sense of tradition, however, is precisely what dulls our senses to the truths we desperately need to live by; we need a new way of seeing the profoundly religious nature of our everyday experience. Only the creative person—and by this I do not mean the bizarre and pseudo-creative individuals who sometimes pass themselves off as the real thing—can dip into the hidden levels of his or her own consciousness as well as that of the human race. They understand the language of faith in a way that allows them to translate it so that we can all comprehend and speak it better ourselves.

This is not a luxury or a fascinating and colorful hobby for some interested people; it is a necessity if we are to meet the demands of the human need to believe. The trouble is that you cannot give orders to or supervise the work of creative persons; you can only, as Alexander the Great learned from Diogenes, stand out of their light. No wonder the creative person has so often had a difficult time with organized religion; it has always tried to harness forces that can only flow freely. Critics of creative people, imagining them to be an untidy and vaguely Bohemian group, forget the intrinsic demands of the authentic act of creation. It demands everything—that "throwing away of the self"—if it is to be successful. As Barron notes, "the artist submits his will to a purpose beyond himself in a manner complete enough for the humblest monk." (Ibid.)

I firmly believe that the men and women who function creatively in theology, especially in its pastoral and liturgical dimensions, should be given as much encouragement as possible at the present time because of what they can do for us in supplying the religious symbolism to nourish our faith. This can be done by no one else. The creative person does not, in a profound and wonderful sense, know what he or she is doing; he knows how to do it and he knows the price of self-surrender that he must pay in order to be successful. It is the instinct of the organizer to ask for five-year plans and projections; these are, of course, what the creative person cannot seriously offer at all. It is the felt obligation of ecclesiastical leaders to keep things like liturgical experimentation under fairly rigid control; they must trust the creative persons in the Church more, allowing them to find their way because they are finding the way for the rest of us at the same time. Picasso was once asked to explain the work of the artist, and in probably as good an answer as he could give, he replied, "To make." When asked just how this process worked, he responded, "Don't talk to the driver!"

I believe in visions but not those of saints from other times as much as those of the persons of creative faith and temperament who help us to see our way into the new age. These visions of our possibilities, cast in the forms and symbols that speak to us now, are indispensable for the vigor of our faith life in Jesus. These creative visionaries are building the Church anew, not in the sense of strange and dreadful novelties as much as in the sense of giving a rebirth to the life-style and sacramental reality of the believing community. They help us to recognize ourselves and each other as well as our ever fresh opportunities to heal and resurrect each other. I think we should believe in these people enough to allow them to make mistakes or occasionally to be obscure in the way they try to speak to us. The final test—and the one we can trust completely—is in the response of the believing community to the pastoral and liturgical forms they provide for us. If these capture the essence of the Gospel in our language, we respond with a new fullness to the religious nature of living; we believe more deeply and recognize the mystery of living in Jesus in the bread they break for us.

We need that believing community with its sure sense of what holds together in terms of its operational faith. I believe in the Church, not only as mystery but also as organization steeped in familiar strengths and weaknesses. I think we need an organized Church to provide the identity for the community of fellow believers who can be so enormously supportive to us as we stand facing the struggles and problems of our individual lives. Our faith needs the voices and the feel of people who believe in us and stay close to us on our long and seemingly lonely journeys. The sacraments are human signs that fit the stages of that journey and these would also be diminished, as would be our recognition of each other, without a gathering of believers to which we can join ourselves. It is in this living community that the richest treasures of the faith have always been generously passed on to others. To mention but one distinctive thing that can only be handed on through the spirit of a community, our sense of sin and its forgiveness constitute an important inheritance. We are born and grow among people with a sense of how they can hurt each other as well as a sense of how, through forgiveness and healing, they can restore that state of possibility that is so fundamental to a living and creative faith.

Related to this are the symbols and rituals that are important for the experience of life. As mentioned before, these symbols, the discoveries of our most creative believers, sound a public, resonating tone for our common religious quest; they enable us to recognize our kinship with each other and

with all people who have preceded us or who will come after us. An organized Church becomes an indispensable
treasury for these, an appropriate housing for the signs and
symbols of living faith as well as a home for the believers
who feed on them.

An organized Church also offers an identity and a unifying tradition for persons of very differing cultural and ethnic
backgrounds. It provides a meeting ground on which they
can recognize each other as human beings without sacrificing
either their language or their heritage. Only an institutional
Church offers us the transcending identity that enables us to
continue to be different while we sense our deep unity in
faith. If we are ever to help human beings to live as brothers—as well as put an end to elitism in religion—it will require something like an institutional Church as a setting in
faith for it.

In the same way the office of pope offers us an invaluable
symbol of unity, a sense of religious awareness that would
be greatly diminished without him. There are layers of tradition that need to be peeled away from the papacy, but the
core notion is one of theological and psychological genius;
it also demands an institution to support it. In the same way,
the organized Church provides a forum for the dialogue of
living faith and, despite noises to the contrary, has a large
capacity for allowing differences of outlook among its members. The Church's capacity for tolerating differing outlooks
is one of its greatest if most underestimated strengths.

These observations have been made about the structured
Church as something that I feel it is important to believe in.
This goes counter to the opinion of many people who despair of an institutional Church ever keeping up with the
needs and experiences of its people. There is inevitable tension involved in keeping the organized Church a believable
phenomenon, but I think that anyone who is seriously concerned about the religious future of mankind must also concern himself with this problem. We need to have faith in the
Church, a creative kind of faith that keeps turning it back

to its possibilities and never lets it rest on its accomplishments or, God help us, on its authority.

I believe in the experiences the Church itself has singled
out as essential for human development; freedom and trust
and enough time to grow. These experiences are familiar to
us but they are seldom granted except by persons who believe enough in others to give these things away to them.
The test of the Church will always be how much it actually
believes in the things it says are good, in the things it can
only give away, in the things that persons need in order to
be able to believe in themselves or in anyone else. These
elements are as basic as air and water to the healthy development of human personality. Giving them away involves us
in a transaction of faith because these things cannot be faked
or otherwise produced artificially; people know the difference right away. Sacrilege might well be defined as that
offense against persons that is committed by others who
offer them the stones of manipulation for the bread of faith.

I believe also in fidelity, as an expression of the profound
mystery through which we work out our salvation in relationship to each other. Only through a commitment to the best
that is in ourselves and in the living experience of good people do we ever forge our way past the letter of the law and
begin to understand the Spirit who gives life to us all. Fidelity, however, is sometimes fragile, and it is often under siege.
It is the special test of how much we are willing to believe
and of how many deaths we are willing to undergo in order
to keep re-creating our lives afresh with each other. The true
Christian can never be bored because he is always impli-
cated in the new discoveries of personality that are made
only by passionate believers. Believing makes us look on each
other as persons; maybe that says everything as briefly as
it can be put. But it is not a simple charge to be nice or to
do good and avoid evil. Looking on each other means to
preserve a vision of what each of us can become—a perception of the possibilities that seem to be lost under the
veil of our shortcomings or failures—and to keep working

through those relationships by which we become ourselves. That is work enough for a lifetime, and even then it will be left unfinished. But belief concerns itself with what is unfinished about us and our world.

That is the crucial mystery at the heart of all our relationships, that arena where we touch and are touched by any hints we will ever get about transcendent meaning. We must keep believing in each other in order to keep our relationship alive; love does not take care of itself and lovers who fail to sense each other's changeableness will soon only remember or sadly mourn their love. I think life—religious life, if you like—is worked through in the way we strive to be faithful and true and loving to each other. That is filled with numberless deaths and rebirths, with the strange and sometimes dizzying experiences that break us out of our own narcissistic jails and give us the chance to celebrate the freedom of God's children together. What use the creeds without this? What meaning in life for the person who has been denied these experiences or who has learned to treat people either as temptations or as tasks to be carried out well in view of a celestial gold star?

I do not believe in faith as something to be hoarded in miserly or fearful fashion. It is inadequate if it is considered only as the light by which we can see others and, through doing self-conscious good to them, add to our bank account of rewards in heaven. Many of us have been victims of this tendency to use faith as an instrument for securing our salvation; we view it, when we are so persuaded, as something that must be clutched and conserved and that cannot be spent freely and lovingly. I am reminded of the old actor, James Tyrone, in Eugene O'Neill's famous play, *Long Day's Journey into Night*. He has been miserly all his life and now, with one son a drunk, the other desperately sick with tuberculosis, and his wife a drug addict, he pauses as he tightens a light bulb he had unscrewed earlier in order to save money, "What the hell was it I wanted to buy, I wonder, that was worth— Well, no matter. It's a late day for

regrets. . . . No, I don't know what the hell it was I wanted
to buy . . ."

Obsessive Christians, fearful of their faith, may find that
they cannot quite remember what they were saving it for
either. Mankind and the world—you and I—need to be believed in here and now, and only faith that is ready to
spend itself without fear that it will exhaust itself is up to
the job. The Christian who timidly performs saving acts of
virtue has not yet understood that he can buy neither happiness nor heaven in such a way. I can imagine nothing
sadder than the supposed believer who kept all the good
news to himself, a marvelous orthodox store, and who now
asks, in the tones of a person who feels he has missed life
somewhere along the line, "What the hell was it I wanted to
buy, I wonder, that was worth— Well, no matter. It's a late
day for regrets . . ."

Life and faith are grander than that truncated conception.
I believe that the Gospels are good news and that we are
barely at the beginning of understanding the person, not
as the naked ape but as the believing animal who can be
believed in. In the long run, that is why I get up in the
morning and lead the life I do. I believe in the human person, and it is not an impossible fancy to think that God does
too. I think it is important to try to understand the person
and to provide for him the conditions he needs to become
fully himself. We are all caught up, I think, in the mystery of
incarnation, in that long pilgrimage, plagued with darkness
and misunderstood directions, by which we move toward
the fullness of ourselves and the fullness of time. We are
saved or lost depending on how much we give or withhold
ourselves from each other along the way.

I believe in love, not abstractly or wishfully, but because
in my own life it has been the experience of love that has
caused me to search myself most deeply and to sort out the
things I believe in from the things I have believed about.
Love sets you on a journey and then gradually transforms
itself on you, bidding you to emerge more from yourself

and to invest yourself more deeply in the life and concerns of another. The journey is, however, the thing; it leads away from living by expectations, pleasing others, or from thinking that faith is found only in ecclesiastical decrees or theological textbooks.

You can love and not examine what you believe in—but you cannot do it for long. You cannot, in fact, love and escape the taste of the deepest and most demanding mystery of the Gospel. That believing in Jesus is tested by our belief in each other and that anyone who believes and loves will find that his experience of life is thereby deepened and transformed. The bells of the scriptures ring clearly in your life when you try to love. What may once have been random events are now understood as the feasts and friendships, the loneliness and separation, the small deaths and resurrections through which we sense the mystery of Jesus in our own lives.

Life does not just happen to us, and as we become aware of our freedom, we grapple with the vexation of an endless series of increasingly difficult choices. I believe the life of the Spirit is something we break into as we break out of ourselves through trying to love more deeply and truly. That is the creative choice that developing faith offers to us each day—to get better at throwing ourselves away—and to know that, finally, this is the way that, gloriously and in each other's company, we find out who we are.